"Your story shows how important it is to have faith, family support, and the best medical team to focus on you as a person. Not all patients are the same, and we have a long way to go, but you are a living example of what's possible."

- Francisco J. Esteva, MD, PhD
Director, Breast Medical Oncology
New York University Langone Medical Center

"Darlene Gore and her daughter have written a poignant account of their family's struggle with cancer that completely touched and then enveloped my heart. For those who have shared similar journeys with cancer, you will be inspired, encouraged, and emotionally renewed as you let their new book bless your life!"

- Sam Haskell
Best Selling Author of Promises I Made My Mother!

"Darlene Gore's story is a realistic and inspirational account of the hope, disappointments, fears, side effects, and daily realities faced by cancer patients and their families. Darlene's experience is also an example that we must always do our utmost to provide cutting edge care for our patients because we never know with certainty who will be a long-term survivor."

- Steven Curley, MD, FACS
Professor and Chief of Surgical Oncology
Baylor College of Medicine

I Have Cancer

I Want to Live

The True Story of an Unlikely Outcome
with Honest and Practical Suggestions for
Those Who Want to Be Supportive

Darlene Arnold Gore

with
Meredith Gore Warf

WESTBOW·
PRESS
A DIVISION OF THOMAS NELSON
& ZONDERVAN

Scripture quotations taken from the New American Standard Bible,
Copyright © 1960, 1962, 1963, 1968, 1971, 1972, 1973, 1975, 1977, 1995
by The Lockman Foundation. Used by permission." (www.Lockman.org)

WestBow Press books may be ordered through booksellers or by contacting:

WestBow Press
A Division of Thomas Nelson & Zondervan
1663 Liberty Drive
Bloomington, IN 47403
www.westbowpress.com
1 (866) 928-1240

ISBN: 978-1-4908-4543-2 (sc)
ISBN: 978-1-4908-4545-6 (hc)
ISBN: 978-1-4908-4544-9 (e)

Library of Congress Control Number: 2014913081

Printed in the United States of America.

WestBow Press rev. date: 8/5/2014

To my husband, Jay, and our two daughters, Meredith and Grace—gratitude fills my heart, and I thank God incessantly for the blessing of family. My parents, siblings, and friends were right with us throughout this time of suffering in our lives; may we always remember what a difference it made as we seek to help others in their time of need.

Blessed be the God and Father of our Lord Jesus Christ, the Father of mercies and God of all comfort, who comforts us in all our affliction so that we may be able to comfort those who are in affliction with the comfort which we ourselves are comforted by God.

—2 Corinthians 1:3–4

Contents

Preface

May 1, 2004—My husband and I were enjoying an engagement party for a friend's daughter, and I recognized that my life was good. Our younger daughter, Grace, was finishing her second year at the College of Charleston, having just competed in the Miss Teen USA contest. Our older daughter, Meredith, had graduated first in her accounting class at Ole Miss and would soon begin work in Lexington, Kentucky, at a major accounting firm. My husband was engaged in a successful law practice, and my work as a Speech-Language Pathologist was in full swing. I had just received an all-clear annual medical examination in Memphis and had adjusted to actually enjoying the empty nest with its many blessings. Life is good. I am fifty and in certified good health. Soon there will be weddings—and grandchildren—and a little slower pace that comes with getting older so that we can enjoy living each day. Yes, life is good.

May 1, 2004, evening—I noticed a sore lump in my left breast. I wondered, *What is that? Can't be much.* I had just had a mammogram and my annual physical a week ago and been assured I was healthy, but I knew I needed to get it checked out.

May 4, 2004—*Cancer!* I had cancer! There were three multi-centric tumors in my breast. Inflammatory ductile carcinoma, I was told. My life had just been completely changed. *How bad is it? What do I do next? I am scared. I want my good life back—the one with the weddings and grandchildren and vacations with my husband.*

May 14, 2004—I was at the best cancer treatment hospital in the world and had just been told the cancer had spread to my liver. I had metastatic invasive ductile carcinoma … and no future. *God, please—I want to live!*

June 26, 2014—I have been slow-dancing with NED (no evidence of any disease) for ten years and am filled with gratitude and wonder at how I have been blessed. The journey has not been easy, but I realize that through my journey, my Creator has blessed me and my family in ways no one could imagine. I realize that I now am given the daily opportunity to share hope to those battling the demons of cancer, and I have a duty and a desire to share hope of life with those who need it. I am *alive,* and I love to dance!

Chapter 1

When Life Suddenly Changes

At 2:00 a.m., I stared at the empty interstate in front of me from the passenger side. There was too much on my mind to think about being tired. My husband Jay was driving, and we had barely spoken since we left Grenada five hours before. This was not because we were mad at each other but because we did not have to say anything; we each knew what the other was thinking. What about our girls? Jobs? Family? Was this going to be the *end?*

I looked over at Jay, and he was focused on the road, looking straight ahead. We'd been married twenty-seven years, and this was the man I fell in love with: focused under pressure, thinking things through, and making the best decisions, leading our family with dignity and integrity. He was solid and strong, but I knew the hurt in his eyes this night.

The nine-hour drive to Houston, Texas was the first time in a day and a half we were still and had time to think. Captivated by a million stars and miles of empty interstate, I played out the battle in my mind: *MD Anderson is going to tell me to have surgery and go home healed, ready to continue my job, being a mom—my life. Or better yet, the doctors in Memphis were mistaken; it's not really cancer, just cysts.* Deep in my mind, I knew the outcome wasn't good.

I'd spent a lot of time on the road. I still do, as I work part-time consulting with schools about children with disabilities and travel around the state of Mississippi. That quiet time in the car is sometimes the only free time I have all day to clear my mind, think, or focus. It often becomes my time of personal worship, a time I can pray out loud to God as He reminds me of our blessings and all He has done for me. But somehow, tonight, things were different.

It was like I was standing at the edge of a cliff that was eroding away, and the only way down, back, or around was to jump into what I could not see. I tried to pray. My older daughter, Meredith, had prayed for Jay and me as we left our home in Grenada with only a few days' worth of clothes. All I could do now was be still and quiet, fighting the overwhelming urge to be afraid minute by minute.

Turning fifty years old wasn't nearly as difficult as I imagined it might be. I was at a really good place in my career, marriage, and family—*such* a good place. Our marriage was at a comfortable place—not that it had ever really been bad. We had just moved into a quieter phase of our lives as empty nesters. Both of my daughters—beautiful, vibrant, incredibly mature Christian women—had graduated high school and moved away to attend college; they seemed quite focused on their education and careers. My husband and I were proud and relieved.

Jay and I would sit together on our back porch swing (one of our favorite spots) at night and listen to the football being played at the ball field not far from our house. We would reminisce about all the frenzied nights we had spent at the ball field, racing from work, just trying to get there on time with one or both of the girls, trying to find that ever-elusive part of a uniform and remember if we were in charge of snacks that night. And then there was piano, band, church, and school activities ... and on and on. For the first time in almost twenty years, the house was quiet.

We missed our daughters, of course, but we'd listen to the ball games from our patio on Friday nights and say, "It was fun, but isn't this great!" I was not devastated that my daughters were moving into adulthood. Quite the opposite. Of course I missed them, but I was excited for them and the many opportunities I knew would come their way.

As we crossed the bridge over the mighty Mississippi, I was reminded of the long, curvy path that brought us to tonight. It is funny how the years seem like milliseconds after they're gone. Twenty-seven years? Had it been that long since I married the love of my life and swore to stand by him "for better or for worse"?

It hadn't even been a week since last Saturday night, May 1, 2004. Jay and I had been to an engagement party. We came home, and I was getting ready for bed when I happened to look in the mirror. There was a bluish discoloration on my left breast. I felt the discolored spot, and it was hard. I immediately thought, *Something is wrong.* But I didn't want to panic and showed Jay, who was also alarmed. I tried to ignore the worry in my mind, so I continued with my routine, went to bed, and then attended church the next day. But I could not keep from thinking, *My life is about to change.* Again, I told myself that I was only being dramatic. *Nothing really could be wrong.*

First thing Monday morning, May 3, I called my gynecologist and voiced my concern. He said, "Well, you were just in my office two weeks ago. You had a normal mammogram, and I did a clinical breast exam, so I know it's nothing. But if you're worried, come on in."

And he was right. I did have a normal mammogram, just as I'd had for the last ten years. In fact, I was diligent about my yearly checkup and mammogram. I could also be quite persistent when it came to my friends' health, encouraging and even pressing my women friends to have yearly mammograms. But the confidence and casual tone in my doctor's voice made me doubt and question my own concern again. As I got in the car to leave for the appointment, I thought, *This is really going to turn out to be a whole lot of nothing.* But Jay insisted, "Go and get it checked out!"

I went into the examining room, laughing and talking with both my doctor and his nurse. I showed them the area of concern, and they felt of it; then they began to try and aspirate (remove fluid, in this case with a needle) because we all just knew it was a simple cyst. It hurt, and nothing would come out of the mass. My doctor and nurse looked at each other. Again, the thought flashed through my mind: *This is serious.* But I still couldn't accept it. After all, I'd always exercised, watched my diet, and had annual checkups. There was no history of breast cancer in my family.

I was alone that day at the doctor's office. I didn't think it was necessary to bring anyone with me, and when my doctor told me I needed to have an ultrasound (another non-invasive diagnostic tool, sometimes called a sonogram), I began to panic. Well, I have that "fixer" type personality (some would call it Type A), and that meant I wanted to have the ultrasound immediately. But my doctor told me it would probably be at least a week before I could get an appointment. I insisted that I couldn't wait that long, so he sent me to wait in the lobby while his staff tried to get me an appointment sooner. He didn't really say a lot to me.

I walked out to the waiting room. My head was swirling, and I began to feel teary. I was panicked and pleaded with the staff of young girls at the front desk, "Please, you've got to get me in this afternoon or tomorrow at the latest." But, truthfully, they were not very kind and didn't seem to care. They were just going about their day, and I'm sure I was just another crying, frightened person; that can be routine at a doctor's office.

As the miles rolled along through Louisiana at about 3:00 a.m., Jay asked if I needed to stop for the restroom or something to drink. I said, "No, let's keep going." I could not get the older lady sitting in the very back of the office out of my mind. She heard me, came and got me, took my hand, and said, "Let's go sit down."

Her name was Evelyn. Just hearing her name gave me some comfort. She reminded me of Mrs. Evelyn Dyer, a dear friend who worked at my dad's drugstore in my growing-up years. We sat down on a bench. I was trembling and still crying when she put her hands on my hands, looked straight in my eyes, and said, "I don't know what's going on or what you found out, but it's going to be okay."

By this time, the front desk staff had managed to schedule an ultrasound appointment for Thursday, in three days (but that seemed eternity). But Evelyn hugged me and instructed me to sit and wait while she went to make some phone calls. She came back a few minutes later and told me I had an appointment for nine thirty the very next morning. *Thank you, thank you, thank you, Evelyn.* It was not until I put this book together that I learned her name means "life." How perfect. Thank you, thank you, Jesus.

During the drive home, I called Jay right away, but I still told him not to worry, that I would get the ultrasound. And then I started thinking about our daughters. Our older daughter, Meredith, twenty-one years old, was in the middle of final exams at the University of Mississippi (Ole Miss), studying to complete her master's degree. Our younger daughter, Grace, twenty years old, a sophomore, was also in the middle of finals at the College of Charleston in Charleston, South Carolina. I didn't want them to know anything. My father had just had a TIA, a mini stroke. I sure didn't want to add to my parents' stress, so I didn't want them to know anything either!

I gave myself a pep talk on the way home and somehow pulled it together. *Darlene, it's nothing. You're not going to make a big deal out of this. Plus if it is something, it hasn't been there long. You've just had a mammogram and clinical breast exam. You're fine.* Jay informed me that he was coming with me for the ultrasound appointment, but I told him there was no need for that.

By nightfall, I was functioning like my old self, and I knew Jay, an attorney, had a deposition the next morning. It was pointless to disrupt his schedule. I convinced him that I could go alone and left for the ultrasound appointment at seven thirty the next morning.

I was driving north. Jay was driving east. He said, "Call me."

It was probably 4:00 a.m. by now, and I could not stop reliving the week's events. Last Tuesday morning could not have come soon enough. As I walked back into the examining room, that voice came back into my mind—the one that said, *This is serious.* Almost immediately, people started to come in, and I could hear whispers and talking. Someone said, "We've got to do a biopsy *today*." And then more doctors came in and looked at the ultrasound. That's when I knew: *This is bad.* I couldn't talk myself out of it being bad anymore.

I called Jay in shock and told him they'd found something, and were getting ready to do a biopsy. Jay said, "I'll get there as fast as I can." They started the biopsy, and that's when they told me there were *three* tumors. Jay was still two hours away.

The biopsies *hurt.* Even though a topical anesthesia was used in the procedure, the doctor had to take ten samples from each tumor—thirty sticks. However, the state of shock I felt blunted a lot of the pain. The nurses and technicians were very kind; they kept asking if I was okay. My body was shaking and trembling on the table, and someone in the room placed his or her hands on my shoulders. I felt like I was in the middle of a whirlwind.

I lay on the table, scared to death and surrounded by medical staff, when a wonderful nurse walked in and said, "Elvis is in the building!" It made me smile, and I knew immediately that Jay had arrived. When the biopsies were finished, I got off the table. I still get very emotional when I talk about this, because Jay was just sitting there, waiting for me in another room by himself. And he tried to smile and be strong, but he had turned white, even around his lips. I remember the look on his face. His normally strong voice was cracking and weak. We didn't say a lot but just held each other tightly. I'm sure we were in shock and knew our lives, as we knew them, would never be the same.

A few minutes later, the radiologist and nurse came in to see us. The doctor said, "We *know* it's cancer. We don't know specifically the type; the biopsies will have to be completed, but it is three tumors, which means it's multi-centric." She explained that this was breast cancer in which there is more than one tumor and that all formed separately from one another, usually in different quadrants of the breast.

The nurse told us she wanted to take Jay and me up to meet the surgeon. I was just in a daze. He was nice enough but very matter-of-fact and to the point. He confirmed that the cancer was multi-centric. He told me I had no choice but to have a mastectomy followed by chemotherapy. He told me he could do the surgery the next Thursday. We scheduled another consultation appointment with him two days after the biopsy results would be complete.

My initial thoughts were, *Thank God we're going to get this cut off and it's going to be gone!*

I rode home with Jay, leaving my car at the hospital, and we began to talk. I was sick, but somehow—and I don't know how—I started trying to get back in a positive state of mind. I was terrified, but I kept saying, "It's going to be okay. We're going back to meet with a surgeon. We have a plan." And then I even hoped and prayed that they were all wrong, it was some huge mistake, and I didn't have cancer after all. I wanted some of my closest friends praying, so after I got home, I called just a few along with the IPM (intercessory prayer ministry) at our church. I was still trying to protect my children while they were taking final exams. I knew they would be horrified by the news.

Some of those closest friends spent the entire next day with me on that long Wednesday of waiting. My friend Irma arrived early, then Elizabeth, Jan, and several others. That day, I didn't want chatter, noise, or really to hear anyone talking. I just wanted the quiet comfort and reassurance of the ones I loved around me.

But at seven o'clock that night, the call came that confirmed what we'd already been told; all three tumors were malignant. The official diagnosis was multi-centric breast cancer, infiltrating ductal carcinoma.

Practical suggestions for friends and supporters when someone has had news like this:

- Be there, and be available.
- Do not talk about treatment or possibilities at this point.
- Just let the person know that you care about him or her; do not ask questions.

"He will cover you with His feathers, and under His wings you may seek refuge; His faithfulness is a shield and bulwark" (Psalm 91:4).

Chapter 2

Holding On for Dear Life

My mind kept wandering in and out of real time that somehow seemed to go in slow motion and at lightning speed at the same time. It was 5:00 a.m. on Friday, and the adrenaline kept revving up. I watched the trees pass on the side of the interstate in a blur as we approached Houston.

I looked over at Jay, and my eyes met his. Even though his ache was hard to hide, I felt the strong, solid, tender heart that I had leaned on through the years and even more now. He did not know any better than I did what was about to happen, but for just a second, I thought, *Okay. It's all going to be okay.* I had to look away quickly to keep from crying. Silence speaks volumes.

How did it come to this? I played it over and over in my mind.

I made the call to Meredith and Grace on Wednesday night after getting the bad news. I felt guilty even telling them. Grace had just finished exams in Charleston, South Carolina and was planning on moving back closer to home to finish her degree at Ole Miss. She had about a week of packing left before we were scheduled to help her move. Meredith had two final exams left in her master's degree at Ole Miss and was packing to leave Oxford and start her career. Both girls tried to be brave. They didn't panic, and with quiet confidence, they told me they were okay and that they loved me. It is so hard to describe what it feels like to know you have just devastated your children and there is nothing you can do about it. It's pretty close to torture.

I had also called my parents, one of the hardest things I've ever had to do. Even though I am fifty years old, I'm still their child. My temperament is to never worry them as an adult and not bother them with things—and now this.

I looked out the car window and saw signs for downtown Houston. It felt like we'd never arrive. I kept reliving the week's events. As long as we were driving, I felt that this wasn't real. The story continued, and maybe if I replayed it again, we'd have an alternate ending and I would wake up from this nightmare. A part of me felt triumphant: we made it in time. The other part quickly dampened the mood, reminding me why we were here in such a hurry. I tried to be thankful at everyone's efforts to help us get here.

Jay, my friends Irma and Jan, and I left at five thirty on Thursday morning. They were driving us since Jay had left his truck in Memphis a few days before and had ridden home with me. I put the CD Meredith had given me the night before in the player immediately and said, "I love you, but I don't want you to talk." They were all very surprised because I usually talk a lot! But I just wanted quiet. The fear was gripping me again, and I wanted to meditate on the words of the music. We listened to that music all the way to the hospital. Every song was relevant, and I cannot begin to explain how much that helped.

Somebody's Praying Me Through
Written by Darrell R Brown and Ty Lacy

Pressing over me like a big blue sky,
I know someone has me on their heart tonight.
That's why I know it's gonna be all right—
'Cause somebody's praying me through.

So when you're drowning in a sea of hurt
And it feels like life couldn't get any worse,
There's a blessing waiting to push back the curse,
'Cause somebody's praying you through.
Somebody's praying you through.

Mom, Dad, and my sister, Gay, met us at the surgeon's office, where the surgeon did a needle biopsy of a lymph node. Since all three of my tumors were cancerous, we needed to know if it had spread to the lymphatic system. If so, the stage of the cancer was more advanced and required a different approach and potentially more than one surgery. This time, it was only a prick and didn't hurt at all. But if the doctors told me it was cancerous, it would change the ball game.

Afterward, we did not know what to say, and the surgeon still maintained the surgery scheduled for the next week. The course of action, he said, was surgery, then chemo and radiation. After a few moments, I began to process what was happening, and my mind started working a little better.

I said, "Wait a minute. Don't we need to see if this has spread to anywhere else in my body? Wouldn't I see an oncologist?" I finally had begun to think and wake up to reality. But the surgeon told me that the mastectomy had to come first, and we would deal with everything else later.

I assured him I was ready to have the surgery as soon as possible. But then I asked again, "How do we know the cancer is not somewhere else?"

He said, "Oh, you're fine. You're fine." And he kept insisting that he would send me to an oncologist after the surgery. He gave me the names of two oncologists and said I would see them after I recovered, probably three to four weeks after the surgery.

The surgeon also kept emphasizing reconstruction, which we kept saying was not a priority to us at this point. We just wanted to get rid of the cancer!

There was a finality in his tone that troubled me—an unwillingness to listen or consider other issues. I thought I saw a red flag. But how did I even know what red flags were in this situation?

And then there was the wonderful nurse who'd escorted us to the surgery suite for our meeting. I could tell that she didn't agree with the surgeon's opinion. She had heard me ask specific, direct questions of the surgeon, and she had heard him brush me off. She was very warm, sweet, and approachable, which is very important when a patient is trying to digest serious health information.

The nurse asked, "Why don't you go ahead and call those oncologists today? I can help you, but why don't you go ahead …" Her voice trailed off, but I knew what she meant. She probably could have lost her job. I'll never forget her. She encouraged me that day without being critical of the doctor.

Jay and I agreed that we wanted a second opinion. We knew several people from our hometown who had received a dire cancer diagnosis, received treatment at MD Anderson, and had good results. We also knew that MD Anderson is a place one goes when a diagnosis falls outside the normal protocol of treatment. Something told me that was the place I was to seek treatment. We asked the staff to call while we were still in the office. MD

Anderson, we were told, was not taking any new patients for six weeks.

And then we left. Our family went to lunch together. I could just barely breathe at that point. *Lord, just show me what we need to do,* I thought. That red flag was the Holy Spirit saying, "You must get a second opinion. You must get a second opinion." I had no peace with what the surgeon wanted to do.

Jay and I left my devastated parents and sister and started the drive home to Grenada at about two that afternoon. "I'm not feeling good about this," I told him. He nodded his head in agreement.

You must get to know us. We're very direct, driven people, independent by nature. That's just the way God made us. Jay and I have a history of butting heads because we each think we're right. It gets loud at our house sometimes. But this time, I think our common stubbornness was a great thing. We were immediately on the same page. We were listening to our intuition, and we didn't like what we'd just heard. In our minds, the surgeon was moving too quickly without knowing the totality of what was going on inside my body. We both thought that in my particular case, the second opinion should come from MD Anderson. We had a one-week window before surgery and had just hit a six-week obstacle. But in my obstinate mind, there is always a way around an obstacle if you are persistent enough. We decided to take action.

On the way home from Memphis, I called my dear friend Irma, who gave me the cell number of her father, Henry P. Mr. P's cousin is a physician who works in Houston, not at MD Anderson. At two thirty, Mr. P answered; he was on a golf course, in the middle of a game, but he answered the phone! Immediately, he called his cousin in Houston (who, as Jay says, "didn't know us from Adam's house cat"), who immediately stopped whatever he was doing at his practice in the middle of the afternoon and made a phone call to a lady. She also didn't know us from Adam's house cat. These people, including two total strangers, immediately stopped what they were doing and took action to help someone.

About an hour later, as we crossed the Yalobusha River Bridge, only ten minutes from our home, we got a phone call from MD Anderson. I had an appointment for eight the next morning! If I could get the tissue slides of the biopsies (which were all ninety miles behind us at the hospital lab in Memphis that closed at 5:00 p.m.), get a bone scan, have a CT of the chest and abdomen, and bring all the results with us, the doctor would come in on his day off and see us at 8:00 a.m. the next day. Houston, Texas is a nine-hour, 565-mile drive from our home.

By then it was 4:00 p.m., and we went into "do it" mode. We called our friend, Elizabeth, whose daughter, Katie, lived in Memphis. Elizabeth called Katie, who picked up the slides, and Elizabeth and Irma met her halfway between Memphis and Grenada, picked those up, and brought them to us. We called our friend, Bart, a radiologist at our hometown hospital, Grenada Lake Medical Center, and he set everything up with radiology and the hospital lab. He kept his staff late, moving heaven and earth to help us. The bone scan and CT, while not painful or invasive, were lengthy. The CT involved drinking two bottles of chalky-tasting contrasting dye and waiting two hours before taking the images. (Since then I've had about twenty CTs. I tell the technicians that they should put umbrellas in them so we can at least pretend they're refreshing Caribbean drinks.)

While trying to maneuver through morning Houston traffic, I repeated the verse from my Bible study that morning: "By my God I can leap over a wall" (Psalm 18:29).

Our daughter, Meredith, came home Thursday night to see us off. As we hugged, just the three of us there in the kitchen of our house, she prayed. "Heavenly Father, we know You have a plan, and for some reason, You have ordained these days. We beg You now for peace, total healing, and supernatural strength that only You can give. Keep Dad's hands steady at the wheel and Mom's hope secure. Keep them strong, Lord. Protect them. *Heal them.*"

The day began at 5:30 a.m. Thursday, and with the sun rising at seven Friday morning, we pulled into the Rotary house across the street from MD Anderson.

Practical suggestions for friends and supporters when someone has had news like this:

- Be there to help. We will never forget the amazing people who, without question, took care of *all* that we needed to leave for Texas that night. They truly saved my life.
- Consider getting a second opinion before deciding on a treatment plan. Do not be afraid to question your doctor; this is your health and body at stake.

"The steadfast of mind Thou wilt keep in perfect peace because he trusts in Thee" (Isaiah 26:3).

Chapter 3

Reality Sets in the Land of Cancer

I felt relieved—almost as if we'd made it to the finish line of a long race. But then I remembered, *I have cancer.* And again, the flood of uncertainty and fear gripped my mind. I kept thinking, *Just put one foot in front of the other; the world is not going to stop because you are sick.*

Walking into the Jesse H. Jones Rotary House International, a full-service hotel dedicated solely to serving the needs of MD Anderson patients and their families, I thought I was stepping onto another planet. At seven o'clock that morning, I had entered Cancerland.

The hotel is owned by the MD Anderson, managed by Marriott International, and connects to the medical center with numerous skywalks. Everyone there has cancer—or so it seems. There are too many bald heads walking around to count. Was I really going to become one of those aliens too? *If I live through it?*

Of course, the clerk at the front desk at the Rotary House didn't understand why we were trying to check in at that time of the morning. Jay and I were utterly exhausted after being up for a day and a half. Our world had changed. After a little explanation from Jay, it was as if the gatekeeper for Cancerland finally understood and let us hurry to a room and drop off our bags.

We walked through the skywalk and into the doctor's office at exactly 8:00 a.m. Not long after, in walked Dr. Esteva—a young, handsome man, slim and tall with dark hair, kind eyes, and a Spanish accent. I liked him immediately, but he was rather quiet, and I wanted him to be more animated on our first visit.

I anxiously handed hand him copies of the bone and CT scans, hoping he'd look at them and immediately say, "Oh, don't worry, all you need is a little *of this.*" He pulled out the discs and looked at them right in front of us. It only took him a few moments to review the films, and I could see the concern on his face.

He was still quiet and didn't say a whole lot. At that point, we didn't even know what to ask. He simply said, "The CT of the abdomen has some spots; we need to check out the liver." He scheduled me for an MRI for five o'clock that very afternoon.

Liver? Wasn't this breast cancer? I replayed those few words he said over and over in my mind all day. Surely this didn't mean the cancer had spread.

Instantly, I liked Dr. Esteva's reasoning. He was calm and steady. I could detect thoroughness in his nature. *Thorough* is what I understood and respected. And I was glad to have the MRI so quickly. After that news and with that uncertainty, *waiting* simply did not fit into the agenda.

He shook my hand and looked straight into my eyes. He told me that the MRI was at 5:00 p.m. and that he and the medical *team* would see me on Monday, and we would probably start chemo on Tuesday.

As I sat in the waiting area for the MRI, I was scared, and in the machine I was scared, even though the test is painless and I'm not claustrophobic. I knew that if the cancer had spread throughout my body, the test would reveal just that. Until the last week, a group of ladies had been attending a Bible study in my home. We were studying Beth Moore's *Believing God* and were encouraged to make little blue bracelets to remind us of the five statements or pillars of faith from that study.

I held onto that homemade blue bracelet in the MRI machine. Even with my poor memory, I could remember and repeated to myself, "God is who He says He is. He can do what He says He can do. I am who God says I am. I can do all things through Christ. God's Word is alive and active in me. I'm *believing* God!" The MRI was the first place I held onto the bracelet and its meaning for comfort—the first of many. Many people, patients and medical staff, would ask me what I was saying, and it gave me pleasure to tell them. I'm sure some wondered what planet I'd come from, holding onto a string bracelet and saying those words with such passion and conviction.

Finally, at 6:30 p.m., after being up for two days, we walked back over to the Rotary House and sat in the big, open dining room. We were troubled, fearful, and exhausted—as Jay would say, "wasted tired." All at once, we heard someone shout, "B 15!" People were playing bingo somewhere nearby. I could not help it and said, "Have we really hit the bingo stage? The only way I'm playing is if I can call out the numbers!" We looked at each other and lost it laughing for the first time in days.

We tried to eat but couldn't eat much. I surely didn't want to *feed* this cancer in my body. We went back to our room, hoping for a little sleep. Jay and I didn't really want to talk. When something grips your life like this, it seems to be the only thing to talk about—and the last thing we wanted to talk about. We sat on the bed there in the hotel room and prayed. Mostly, we begged God for direction and discernment in deciding the best course of treatment. Of course, we prayed for comfort, rest from the fear, and for our girls to stay strong. We tried to sleep, but rest was fractured, restless, and troubled.

Had we really just finished a marathon scavenger hunt? We had to wait until Monday to even find out the results. What were we supposed to do all weekend? Tour Houston? I think not. Of course, we tried to get our minds off the situation all weekend, but how could we? We were staying at the epicenter of Cancerland, and we talked to many others who were there receiving treatment as well. I was very thankful we made it to Houston—after all, we almost didn't.

Mr. P and Adam's two housecats—the three Jewish angels, as I affectionately call them—truly changed the game for us. God's hand was on them—on us. Each of them acted immediately on our request for help and made a simple phone call. If the chain of events had changed, if anyone had delayed the call, if doctors and their staff had not made huge efforts to administer the tests required before I could see Dr. Esteva, I would not be here.

Timing was critical. We knew that, but we didn't yet know *how* critical.

Practical suggestions for the impact of reality:

- Always try to find humor in the situation.
- Boldly pray.

"Let us therefore draw near with boldness to the Throne of Grace, that we may receive mercy and may find grace to help in time of need" (Hebrews 4:16).

Chapter 4

The Rainbow

Mother's Day: May 9, 2004
With Meredith, Grace, Darlene, and Jay

Meredith and Grace are two of the greatest gifts God has given me. I have always prayed for them—their health, the path God would put them on, and that they would find godly men as well as their overall well-being. But this Mother's Day would be different. They would be the ones wanting to watch over me.

Being in Houston with the present circumstances was hard enough, but as a mother, I didn't want to share this burden with my children. Of course, I wanted to shield them from what was going to be a painful, scary, and uncertain journey. More than anything, I was thankful this was happening to me and not my girls.

I have known friends whose precious children have been afflicted with this terrible disease and cannot imagine anything worse. My *hair* hurts to think of my children going through anything painful, emotionally or physically. At least I've lived a full life for fifty years. Mothers are willing to go through anything in order to shield their children from pain, suffering, and sickness.

Little did I know that after my last conversation with them, they hopped in the car and were on their way to see me. I'd told them not to come. Like their mother, they can be determined when they make up their minds about something. I cannot imagine the unanswered questions and fears that must have played through their minds as they drove the long hours to Houston. Thoughts of weeks, months, and years to come quickly change with the simple word *cancer*. As terrifying as the situation is, I believe that my girls, like myself, held on to simple promises of faith that far outweigh the afflictions of the present.

While thinking of these things and how to have a life in Houston, I was surprised when the girls walked in. My two stubborn angels where there to celebrate Mother's Day with me, and for a moment, I could rest, knowing we were all together.

> **Meredith:** After Mom has incessantly demanded that we *not* drive to Houston for the weekend, of course, Grace and I hopped into the car and started driving. We didn't really talk much on the nine-hour drive, just sort of stared at the road ahead. I don't even think we stopped to eat. How could we *not* spend Mother's Day with our mom, especially when she'd been handed such a devastating diagnosis? We pulled into the Rotary House, which would become such a familiar place that year yet such a sad place at the same time.

In spite of everything, it was truly a wonderful day. We'd attended Beth Moore's Sunday school class at First Baptist, and I'd realized that if I stayed in Houston, what a blessing it would be to sit in her class. We all went for a nice lunch, back to the hotel room, and were trying to fill the silence with small talk. I say small talk because I was dreading the big talk—the "where do we go from here" talk.

After a little time had passed and we'd flipped through all the channels on the television what must have been seven times, I felt that nudge to talk to the girls about what was happening to me, to all of us. It hurts me now to think about their faces, how strong they were trying to be for Jay and me.

I simply said, "Let's talk about all of this a minute," and they both began to cry. I'm sure they needed to cry. I knew what I said would make a tremendous impact, and I prayed for the right words. I knew this moment was critical for my children's well-being for the rest of their lives. God came through in a big way because I was crying but calm. I told them how much I loved them and how God had blessed me with a wonderful husband and two amazing, wonderful daughters. I stressed how thankful I was for them and my life on this earth.

God was right there with us in the stillness as I reminded them that Scripture tells us that our days on this earth are ordained before we are ever born. God knows exactly how long we will be here, and if this was my time to leave this earth, they had to believe His words. I told them that we were seeing the best doctors and doing all we could do to fight, but the final determination of time would be His. He alone anoints our days. By this time, we were all crying and hugging. They each said, "I know."

Trying to be strong for them was the only way I could hold it together. Of course, I didn't want them to leave because then I'd have to look in the mirror and fight the overwhelming threat of fear. Talking about the right things doesn't mean I felt them, but I was doing my best to believe what I was saying.

> **Grace:** Now that I'm married, I cannot *imagine* sitting side-by-side, holding Micajah's hand with a strong face and, without crumbling, telling our children about this kind of diagnosis in the way they did. I remember Mom sitting quietly, sometimes bowing

her head, sometimes looking at us. Dad's voice shook a little when he talked to us.

The exact conversation is hazy now, probably a purposefully suppressed memory. I can still close my eyes and look around that room and see us all—our faces, the uncertainty, the fear. Looking back, there has never been a more intimate, [close], bonding family moment for the four of us—mother, father, daughters. We never came right out and talked about the odds that Mom would not make it through this thing, but Mom and Dad talked about how God would get us through, no matter the outcome; that He never gives more than we can bear; that we'd be strong for each other and to glorify Him through this battle.

Meredith: And for the first time, we all really talked about the reality of the situation. None of us had vocalized everything we'd been thinking, much less let our emotions go and cry.

Mom said it for the first time: "You know, girls, it *is* going to be okay. I am okay if this is the end for me. I will fight this with everything I have, but we all have a time here which is just temporary." At that point, I was almost mad at her for saying those words. We were to never give in to defeat, never surrender a battle, and never accept failure. I think I was picturing death from cancer as failure. Boy, I had a lot to learn! It was like her saying the words made her death actually possible. I was refusing to believe that death, that finality, was one of the multiple choice answers laid out before us—that we didn't have a choice.

All four of us sat in a pile of hugs and held hands as Dad led us in prayer. "The Lord is my Shepherd. I shall not be in want." Oh, how we all wanted so much that afternoon. He prayed for our peace and comfort and strength through this journey and prayed that we would glorify Him throughout the entire process.

He also prayed for God's will to be done, and if it be so, grant us more days with Mom. But during that aspect of the prayer, I zoned out, again refusing to believe anything except this whole thing just going away—denial. Deep down, we all knew this might be the last Mother's Day hug with Mom here on this earth, the last time we all four piled up in the bed like this—last this, last that.

Grace: The most heart-piercing part of the conversation truly was Mom reminding us that God has preordained each of our days—that we are to take life and the things that come that are completely out of our control [and] live our best for Him, realizing that He already knows the beginning and the end for each of us. I didn't know if the tears would stop. I wanted to just wake up from this dream.

Afterwards, we all piled on top of the bed in that room, all snuggled so close. We had the Jeff Foxworthy *Blue Collar Comedy Tour* on video in the room and decided to put it in. After all the emotion of that day, that silly redneck show brought each of us laughter. We laughed and laughed and laughed, cuddled up on top of that bed together.

When we left the room, I'd started to tear up again and walked the other way down the hallway by myself to pull myself together. At the end of the hallway, I took hold of the windowsill, not knowing what was going to happen to us but knowing that we were entering a huge season of change and pain. Mom was close behind me. We looked out the window, and there was the most beautiful, perfect rainbow I've ever seen in my life. We called to Dad and Meredith, and they walked down to where we were. We all stood there for a moment, looking at that rainbow.

I know without a doubt in my heart that just as God used the rainbow biblically as a reminder of His promises, He did that for me—for our family. No matter the outcome, God has promised us that He will always be in control. I knew in my heart that this pain and fear would not last forever. To this day, rainbows take on a whole new meaning. God keeps His promises. And He gave us a big, giant, beautiful rainbow to remind us when it was so hard to remember.

Meredith: It had been raining cats and dogs when we pulled into Houston and most of the day. I didn't even notice the sunshine outside, but Mom did. One of the things I've always admired about Mom is her optimism.

Mom turned around, looked out the window at the end of the long hall, and started walking towards Grace, calling to the rest of us, "Look, y'all ..." We all turned around and saw a magnificent rainbow—huge, clear, and beautiful against the bright sunshine—that actually made the light rays spill through the window into the hall. I could tell Mom and Grace were so encouraged. I tried to be just as comforted by the sign from God but was so caught up in processing the information silently that I really missed the importance.

I do remember thinking, *Rainbows signal the end of the storms, so maybe things will be calming down.* Little did I know the storm was just starting.

Jay: It was a magnificent moment at a time when we were all just flat with the weight of the situation. When you are just grasping for hope wherever you can find it, determined to be positive about a dismal situation, even though you may feel it is really just folly, a drowning man will grasp a straw on the water! It takes a storm to reflect a rainbow.

The rainbow was probably one of the first signs of hope for our family. And we had no idea how soon and how strong we were going to have to hold on to that sign. We thought we'd already heard the worst news, but the worst was yet to come.

Practical suggestions for you and for friends and supporters at this time:

- Talk about what is happening with your family; openly communicating presents the opportunities to pull together and express fears, concerns, desires and options.
- Be emotionally available; be real.
- Do not deny what is going on.

"And it shall come about, when I bring a cloud over the earth, that the rainbow shall be seen in the cloud and I will remember

My covenant, which is between Me and you and every living creature of all flesh" (Genesis 9:14–15).

"Your eyes saw my unformed body; all the days ordained for me were written in your book before one of them came to be" (Psalm 139:16).

Chapter 5

Waiting for Patience

Needless to say, we didn't sleep well all weekend. I tried my best to avoid dwelling on the situation, almost pretending we were on a little mini-vacation to Houston. And sadly, like every other week of the year, Monday comes after Sunday. I returned for medical test results.

It turned out to be another dark day as the MRI revealed two spots on the liver that needed to be biopsied. This meant chemo had to be postponed until after the biopsy results. I felt like I was just pushed back three steps—forward two, back three. Thankfully, the CT-guided liver biopsy was scheduled for the next day. But this raging disease would get another day to eat away at my body. At this point, the only thing I wanted to do was start treatment! If I couldn't have surgery to remove the cancer, the next best thing was chemo to kill the cancer. All this waiting, none of which was on my agenda, was doing the worst thing imaginable: nothing.

Even though we didn't know when chemo was going to begin, the next step in preparation for the treatment was the insertion of a central venous line or a CVC (central venous catheter, an intravenous catheter placed into a large vein in my chest). The

CVC is a direct line for giving patients fluids or long-term medications—in my case, chemotherapy drugs. I was scheduled to get the line Tuesday morning.

The surgeon told me it would help the insertion and lesson my pain to drink water before the procedure, so Monday night, I drank 130 ounces! I didn't even feel the insertion because I had to go to the bathroom so badly. As soon as he got the line in, I said, "Thank you. I gotta run!"

I kept telling myself it would be fine. My wonderful parents were on their way to Houston from Tennessee after I called them to tell them about the biopsy. I've said many times, "Thank goodness it was me and not one of my children." Well, I'm *their* child, and I can only imagine how they felt.

On Tuesday afternoon, we were disappointed to find out the biopsy couldn't be performed as scheduled because there was a backlog of scans already scheduled in CT. Waiting for a biopsy in that modality now meant waiting until the end of May! Instead, the staff did a consult to see if a biopsy could be done with ultrasound, and it was rescheduled in that department for May 17, the following Monday. I fought the urge to beg for an earlier appointment. This meant waiting *another* six days—six more days for this awful cancer to wreak havoc on my body.

In the meantime, Jay learned to do dressing changes of the protective bandagelike covering over the central line. It's a sterile process in which the line is cleaned, flushed, and maintained. The procedure takes about fifteen minutes and has to be performed every three days unless the dressings get wet; then it has to be changed immediately, as we all know that a damp area is a breeding ground for bacteria. Because the procedure has to be done so often, caregivers are trained to complete the dressing changes whenever possible; otherwise I would have to go to the hospital's outpatient department.

I was a nervous wreck during the dressing changes because the staff had instilled in us a fear of the frightening consequences of infections like staph. And patients with compromised immune symptoms can quickly become septic—infection runs rampant throughout the body via the bloodstream. I was told that more patients died of infections than any other complication while in cancer treatment, so I resolved this would not be the case for me.

The line didn't hurt; it was just extremely annoying sometimes. I had to be careful changing clothes, taking a shower, getting hot in the Houston summer heat, and even using my arm, all to protect my lifeline in my chest. As I looked in the mirror daily to put on make-up and fix my hair, I couldn't help but think, *This is the same person I saw in the mirror two weeks ago. I looked just like I did before the lumps appeared, except maybe a little tired. I can't be a cancer patient. My hair is still here; there's no wheelchair, no hospital bed. Am I really sick?* But then I'd see the line. The central line was hidden under my clothes and was the only real proof that I had cancer. I felt fine aside from the new elephant in the room.

I had no idea when the line was inserted that it was going to stay in for eight and a half months. It has been *ten* years now, but I *still* rejoice every day, especially when I'm in the shower, washing my hair, that it's no longer there. The CVC is a small issue in the overall scheme of chemo and its side effects, but it's another tough thing that anyone in treatment has to deal with on a daily basis. One day, I wanted to wash my hair. I covered the site and was very careful, but then after I'd finished, the dressing was wet. It had to be changed immediately. I cried.

I was nervous any time the dressings were changed, as I was aware of the danger of infections, but I was particularly anxious when Jay was in charge. *Ha!* And it was probably only because he didn't seem nervous at all. He was as confident and steady with a central line as he was in the middle of a deposition. I drove him crazy with constant questions like, "Are you sure you didn't touch that? Are you *sure*?" But Jay knew I was nervous, and he was patient with me. What is love?

But even in love, obligations still exist, and Jay had to return home for work and school. The girls had to move out of Oxford and Charleston. Meredith was going to work in Canada for the summer, and Grace was unsure of her summer plans. It was very hard to see them go, but as parents do, my mom and dad (affectionately known as Mop and Pop) came in as reinforcements. Mop had a really hard time looking at the CVC, though I wouldn't know just how much until years later. As a mom, I truly understand; I know how I'd feel if it'd been Grace or Meredith. Still, she and Pop were upbeat and positive with me even though they struggled emotionally.

As the days passed and we waited for the liver biopsy, I began what would end up being the highlight of every day: checking the mailbox. Friends had begun to send cards, e-mails, and gifts. It was truly amazing and humbling. A friend of Mop's sent me *A Bend in the Road* by David Jeremiah, renowned pastor and author. The book is about real people's battles in life—loss of a child or a spouse, struggling with a terminal illness, and Jeremiah's own fight with cancer. The book is filled with Scriptures from Psalms and how those biblical truths apply to us today in our battles. These were just the words I needed to read, and the timing could not have been more perfect.

I was anxious but relieved to see Monday, May 17. Finally, maybe we could get something done about this cancer. At the same time, this meant facing the reality that I may not only have breast cancer, but also cancer in my liver. Telling myself all was going to be okay, I tried to focus on staying calm and prayed for steady emotions.

All went as scheduled that morning. I was prepped for the procedure and chose to remain awake and use a local anesthetic. This was not a good idea. (Note to self: next liver biopsy, choose sedation!) My abdomen was cleaned, and the ultrasound head and gel were positioned to look at my liver. The doctor probed around with an ultrasound and needle to get the sample. It was extremely painful. I felt a lot of pressure and pain, but I remember thinking that it didn't matter as long as the spots on my liver were benign. I tried to focus on remaining still because I knew if the doctor couldn't get adequate samples, then I'd have to be put to sleep so a more invasive technique could be used. I didn't want to waste any more time. I wanted to get started with treatment—to fight!

Afterward, we returned to the game that we were learning to play: waiting. Again, waiting really hasn't ever been on my agenda, and it was the last thing I felt like doing at this point.

The following day, my parents attended the meeting with Jay and me to hear the plan of attack from Dr. Esteva. I already knew that I'd be starting chemo that day, and I felt kind of relieved. I was looking forward to chemo because I was ready to *fight*.

The waiting room was about half full that morning. Some people were obviously undergoing treatment; others were there for family or friend support. The news station broadcasted the headlines of the morning on two flat-screen televisions: the newest from Al-Qaeda and the war in the Middle East, a bomb blast in Baghdad, South Africa winning the World Cup, and the new couple, Brad and Angelina. It was funny how the world kept going, day in and day out, regardless of how I felt or my life as I knew it ending.

We didn't have to wait long, and it's a good thing. I knew the news we would get would be epic. It would determine not only my treatment, but also my prognosis. Thankfully, MD Anderson continued to stress that each case was different and warranted specific evaluation from the medical team. My name was called, and Jay, Mop, Pop, and I jumped up to hurry into the office. Dr. Esteva was quick and to the point.

Dr. Esteva said, "I guess I'm going to have to be the one to tell you …"

I looked at him. I looked at my parents. I wish they'd not been in the room that day.

There were tears in his eyes when he continued, "It has spread to your liver. You are no longer a candidate for surgery."

"I will lift up my eyes to the mountains from whence shall my help come? My help comes from the Lord who made heaven and earth" (Psalm 121:1–2).

Chapter 6

Still Waiting for ... Something

"Not a candidate for surgery?" We couldn't understand why we couldn't get the cancer *out* first and then do whatever chemotherapy, radiation, or other treatment was necessary to get the rest of the cancer. As if they'd done it a million times before, the team patiently and confidently explained that without the tumors, there was no barometer of progress with the chemo. Tumor shrinkage was the best way to make sure the right combination of drugs was used. The logic made perfect sense.

In addition to the three tumors in my breast, there were also three tumors on my liver, and I thought, *They can't even treat me.* I knew then my prognosis had dropped dramatically since the cancer had traveled throughout my body and landed in another organ. I knew it meant I was stage four—end stage. We were devastated.

I felt numb and defeated for a few moments before my Type A, take-charge personality turned on autopilot to ask the hard questions. "What is next ... percentages ... time remaining ..."

Chemo was the next step, and Dr. Esteva told us that I would need to stay in Houston for the duration so that they could monitor the treatment and quickly change the type of chemo if it was not working. He was clear that there were no protocols for Stage IV breast cancer.

Without hesitating, Jay said, "Oh yeah, she'll stay here."

I asked that question that everyone wonders about regarding my prognosis. They never gave a percentage and explained that only some live; the rest die. We asked over and over, but they emphasized that every case is different and "We don't give percentages." Later on, we did what we knew we shouldn't: we looked online. That's where we saw that I had about a 2 percent chance of survival for a year—on or off chemo.

Dr. Esteva grabbed my hand, and I thought, *Okay, this is it. I'm going to die.* I'll never forget what he said; his words were the same words Evelyn had spoken. He did not want to say it, and it was probably against protocols, but he was compassionate and sincere. He looked at me and said, "Darlene, it's going to be okay."

After Dr. Esteva had delivered the news, I asked for the strongest, most aggressive chemo possible and that we get started immediately. He assured me that was what had to be done.

I wanted everyone in the room—Mop, Pop, Jay, and my girls—to hear and know that I was going to fight, that if I didn't make it, I had done everything possible, that I didn't just give up. That strength could have only come from the Lord. He'd been preparing me. The words from Psalm 18:29 floated like one of those planes pulling banners at the beach: "By my God, I can leap over a wall."

I looked at my dear parents and Jay. I kept thinking and wishing they didn't have to hear this news, but at the same time, I knew I couldn't do it without them.

Pop: We'd planned a big celebration that night to celebrate "just" breast cancer. They'd said there was a little spot on Darlene's liver, but we just thought they were wrong and that if the cancer wasn't in her liver, she'd get over it. And then they told us …

Mop: I would've fallen apart. But Darlene just sat there because she was as shocked as everybody when the doctor told us there was cancer in her liver. She had a notebook and a pen with her, and she sat there with tears rolling down her cheeks, taking notes during the whole thing. Taking notes. I was thinking, *How can you sit there and take notes when the odds are you're not going to make it through this?* I thought, *How on earth will I lose my child? And what will she have to go through before she dies?* That's what all I thought.

Grace and Meredith were both at home in Grenada, waiting together for the news of the biopsy. They were very nervous but tried to be positive. We called our staff at church to send someone to be with them as we told them the bad news because I couldn't stand the thought of them hearing the news alone. It meant so much to us that our pastor, youth minister, and choir leader were able to be with them to sort through the news and pray with them. As the word got out, more people came to the house to show love to our children. It was just another example of the love and support that can be found in small-town America. It's a blur now, the memory of that night, but I remember how upset they were on the phone and how they tried to be strong. It was a tough night.

Meredith: I had just gotten home from a run—my escape, outlet, think tank. When I came in the back door, my phone rang—Mom. I think somehow, I knew it wasn't good. I tried to be strong for her. We all know Mom is always okay if her daughters are okay. She must have already called our church staff because people started filing in as soon as we hung up. There may be downsides to living in a small town where everybody knows everybody's business, but oh, what blessings come from so many friends when you let them hold you up.

Jay: One of the first things I remember saying to Darlene was that we [were] not going to question why God had allowed this to happen to us. We were not going to allow the thought that He was punishing us to enter our thoughts, even for one second. Life had given us a choice—fight with all we had or accept an early death. I, for one, certainly don't want to ask God for his grace when I'm mad at Him, and believe me, you need all the help you can get from the only One who can actually determine the outcome—not much of a choice for either of us Type As. For once, the personality traits that had caused us many high-volume discussions were harnessed to pull together for a common goal. A diagnosis of cancer, especially stage four, brings trivial issues people disagree over into focus and reduces them to a nothingness. With that diagnosis, we just dropped everything, prayed, and focused a war against the evil monster that had attacked our family with intent to kill.

Practical suggestions for waiting friends:

- Be there for family members.
- Send cards, e-mails, and text messages.
- Pray.

The Lord is my shepherd; I shall not want. He makes me lie down in green pastures; He leads me beside the still waters. He restores my soul; He leads me in the paths of righteousness for His name's sake. Yea, though I walk through the valley of the shadow of death, I will fear no evil; for You are with me; Your rod and Your staff, they comfort me. You prepare a table for me in the presence of my enemies; You anoint my head with oil; My cup runs over. Surely goodness and mercy shall follow me all the days of my life; and I will dwell in the house of the Lord forever. (Psalm 23)

Chapter 7

Marching into Battle with Chemotherapy

When you pass through the waters, I will be with
you; and through the rivers, they shall not overflow
you. When you walk through the fire, you will not be
scorched, nor will the flame burn you. For I am the
Lord your God, the Holy One of Israel, your Savior.
—Isaiah 43:2–3

Dr. Esteva and the rest of the team had decided upon a plan
of attack, and *finally,* on May 19 at around 7:30 p.m., I began
chemo. The last forty-eight hours had been a blur.

The plan was to hit me with FAC, a chemo cocktail of
Fluorouracil, Adriamycin, and Cytoxin. Some people call
Adriamycin the "red devil," but I didn't want to call it that because
I was thankful it was killing the cancer cells. It was better for
me mentally to view the drugs as a positive force, like a soldier
fighting for my life. I'd read books about the power of positive
thinking, and now it was time to put it to practice. I tried to be

brave for my family, and I kept telling Dr. Esteva, almost like a boxer in the ring, "Come on! Come on! Give me the strongest you've got!"

The chemotherapy infusion room was bare and cold. I hopped up on the treatment table, trying to be calm and remembering what I had read in the pamphlet: drink plenty of water. *Check.* Take anti-nausea medicine before the appointment. *Check.* Eat ice chips to help with possible mouth sores. *Check.* Remain relaxed and calm. *Yeah, right!*

It was hard to stay calm as three of the most powerful toxins that can be injected into the human body flowed from the bag through the tube in my chest. This cocktail was administered over about a two-hour period, then via a pump for four continuous days, another two-hour bolus, then off seventeen days, and then repeat. I took eight rounds. (The word "rounds" is cancer lingo because the eight rounds could take more than six months and for some people up to eight or nine months, depending upon how the chemo is tolerated.)

The television was on, but I didn't want to watch or talk about anything. I thought that if I lay there, closed my eyes, and focused really hard, the chemo would work better! Meredith, her boyfriend Bruce, and Grace were with me, and I told them that the chemo was like Pac Men eating the cancer cells. We all laughed cautiously, hoping it was a quick arcade game.

After a lengthy training on the chemo pump, I left the infusion therapy department around 10:30 p.m. that first night with the fanny pack of the red devil. The treatment was truly okay; I only felt some tingling around my nose. I was very thankful that the battle against cancer cells had begun. The nurses at the chemo center laughed at me; they said they were more used to attitudes of fear and dread because of the side effects. But I was very happy to start the chemo. At last, *action.*

By this point, I had also made a decision to be the most compliant patient possible. If you've never been compliant before in your entire life, chemo is a *critical* time to begin. It'd been explained to me, quite clearly and convincingly by my doctors, that my participation and cooperation were vital to my treatment. People often mistakenly think, as I once did, that the patient is given chemo and then sent home to recover from the drug in his or her recliner. Nothing could be further from the truth. There are a host of side effects that accompany chemotherapy, but the good news is that many are quite manageable and tolerable as long as you are educated, proactive, and organized.

I'm a fairly organized person, but I quickly realized it would be necessary to develop a strict daily routine to help manage the side effects of chemo, to do my part in staying as healthy as possible. I found a routine was not only vital to the effectiveness of treatment and the way I felt, but also that there was a very real physiological payoff. Adhering to a routine, staying as informed and organized as possible, and doing everything I possibly could to feel good in a bad situation gave me back a small sense of control. Don't get me wrong; I knew my life was in the hands of God and my incredible team of doctors, but I was sure going to do everything I could to help out!

I was well advised by the staff and given an enormous amount of reading material and a guidebook to help me navigate chemo. But even with all of that information, I found out about some side effects the hard way. The medical staff's main focus is treatment—keeping the patient alive (as it should be)—and they simply can't advise the patient of every possible side effect.

The only immediate side effect following the first dose of chemo was a headache the next day that lasted until about 2:00 p.m. I was pretty thankful that was all. I felt like the real pressure washing had begun—that the chemo was going to clean out the cancer and flush it from my body. It helped me to visualize the fight that way. And then Meredith sent an e-mail home to Grenada that said, "Please. My mama needs a fight song because she keeps singing, 'The ants go marching in one by one. Hoorah. Hoorah.'"

On the third day of my first chemo treatment, I really began to feel the effect of the nausea. I kept telling myself to *Hold on a little longer; round one is almost over.* Like in a boxing match, I waited for the bell to sound to end the round and just hoped I'd hear, "Darlene, one. Cancer, zero." I'd rest in my corner and gather the fortitude to begin again. It really hadn't been *that* bad. Bruce, Meredith, and Grace were still with me and weren't going home until the round was over and Jay flew in.

I was getting in the bed early that evening with quite a bit of nausea and hadn't felt like eating much supper. Trying to be strong for the girls and Bruce, I'd slipped into bed, hoping to sleep until it was time for pump to be disconnected the next day. Meredith had left to run a quick errand, and Bruce quietly knocked on my door, asking if I was asleep yet. He kindly entered the room and said he had something to show me. About a month earlier, Bruce had talked to Jay and me about proposing to Meredith. I opened up the box. The ring was absolutely beautiful, and he was very excited. So was I, but I couldn't express my joy adequately because I was so focused on not throwing up on the ring!

After Bruce left the room, I tried with all my might to keep from crying. I wanted to be there to see her walk down the aisle.

The nausea was worse when I woke up on the fourth day, but I was glad the pump was going to be disconnected that night. The girls had to leave to fly home with me sick; that was scary and hard for all of us. I just wished I could be stronger for them.

My friend, Jan, flew in Sunday afternoon when Jay had to leave to go back to work, and I tried to rally but gave in to the sickness.

42

Monday was much better, and by Tuesday and Wednesday, I felt so energetic that I even had trouble sleeping! The nurse explained that it could be due to the chemo. Jan's family and our family were the best of friends; we all had grown to be family over the last ten years. I will never be able to describe what a friend she proved to be through this journey.

Jan is a nurse, and I wasn't so nervous about the CVC dressings with her around. Everyone should have his or her own nurse for a friend. She even washed my hair. After covering up my port site and leaning over the tub, she began to gingerly, softly massage my head to wash my hair. I kept telling her to "Wash it good! It might be several days before I can wash it again." I caught her eye and realized what she was thinking: it would be falling out soon. Tears began to run down both our cheeks, but then we couldn't help but laugh!

Moving through Cancerland was like traveling through a foreign country. Everything is different. The people looked different in hospital gowns or clothes that are as comfortable as possible. No power suits exist in Cancerland. It's full of good people and hurting people from all over the world—all colors and ages, some still with hair, some without. Some bear the scars, literally and figuratively, of their battle. The Rotary House, where I stayed the first month, is connected to the hospital, and everybody there shares an invisible, unspoken language. No matter how sick or worried, everybody understands each person there is in the same boat. It's the most incredible thing; mutual sympathy and caring exist among total strangers. You aren't there as a tourist, and everybody knows it.

Every single day, as I continued to battle the fear, loneliness, and depression, I began to feel the tangible uplift of support from many people. It was truly humbling. The more I fought and didn't give in, the more I heard from old friends, high school and college, and from some people I didn't even know—people who reached out to me simply because I was on the prayer list at their church or they knew one of my friends or family members. This was before the age of Facebook, Caringbridge, and social media.

During high school, Meredith and Grace went on a mission trip to Venezuela. Grace got an e-mail from a young man there saying that his entire church was praying for our family! Her college friend, Tim Creager, was serving in Iraq and said his whole unit was praying there. People were praying all over the world! Through the cards, letters, gifts, e-mails, and even caramel cakes, I leaned on those expressions of God's love for me. John 13:34–35 now has new meaning to me: "A new command I give you: Love one another. As I have loved you, so you must love one another. By this everyone will know that you are my disciples, if you love one another." Thank you, friends, for showing me Christ even when it was difficult to see Him.

I will never forget one card. Near the end of June, I received a letter from a dear older lady who lived across town in Grenada. I read it over and over again.

She told me she knew she had not spelled my name right, "But God knows who you are." And then she told me I was on her "midnight prayer list." She said, "This is what we do when circumstances overwhelm us. Let's you and I pray for your circumstances, for we know God answers our cry." She signed the letter, "Love always, Your Friend from across town."

It was overwhelming, humbling, and unbelievably comforting to be on someone's midnight prayer list. Mrs. Louise Hubbard was a political activist in the Civil Rights movement. Midnight prayer was reserved in her society for the most intense focus and emphasis, because you really meant it. I just thanked Jesus for reminding me that somebody was praying me through and thanked Louise for allowing God to use her to show love to me.

Since my arrival at MDA, I'd not sent the first e-mail to any of my friends or family. I was focused on the fight. Jan coordinated an e-mail list that probably included a thousand contacts—a massive effort. She took great care to inform people of my progress (or lack thereof) and any specific prayer needs, things I hadn't the energy to talk about or even begin to organize. I wouldn't find out until later how difficult it was to send the news out; we all shed many tears thinking about what *might have been*.

The night of Tuesday, May 25, I couldn't sleep, so I began reading *A Bend in the Road* by David Jeremiah, a mind-altering book about his cancer journey that Mop's friend had sent. The message I found within its pages was very powerful to me. The next day, I had an overwhelming desire to send a message home to my friends in Grenada. I wanted the people I loved to hear my voice, to let them know I was still very much alive. I also wanted to share something that had profoundly helped me put my situation in a sort of perspective. I figured others might need that message as well.

> Dear Prayer Warriors,
>
> Thank you for all the wonderful, encouraging e-mails and cards and especially for your prayers! I had a scare yesterday when I was told to get a prescription for a cranial prosthesis; when I discovered they were talking about a wig, I settled down. Ha! Hair is the least of my concerns right now, but for the sake of my family and friends, I will get the prescription filled!
>
> The doctor wants me to stay in Houston for a few months in case they change the type of chemo I'm receiving. I'm singing fight songs the four days of chemo to assist with the killing of cancer cells. If you know any good ones, please send. Ha! They are monitoring blood counts the next couple of weeks, and so far, all is well.

Please continue to pray for my complete healing. I
have faith and believe that God can do this. In the wee
hours of the morning, I read a passage from *A Bend in
the Road* by David Jeramiah that truly encouraged me
and warmed my heart. If you've just experienced pain
in your life, or as they say, a disruptive moment, or if
you are going through a crisis at this time, I hope this
will encourage you also:

"There is no music in a 'rest', but there is the
making of music with it. In our whole life-melody, the
music is broken off here and there by 'rests' and we
foolishly think we have come to the end of a tune. God
sends a time of forced leisure, sickness, disappointed
plans, frustrated efforts and makes a sudden pause
in the choral hymn of our lives ... but how does the
musician read the 'rest?' See him beat the time with
unvarying count and catch up the next note true and
steady, as if no breaking place had come between. Not
without design does God write the music of our lives.
Be it ours to learn the tune, and not be dismayed at
the rests. They are not to be slurred over, not to be
omitted, not to destroy the melody, and not to change
the keynote. If we look up, God Himself will beat the
time for us. With an eye on Him, we shall strike the
next note full and clear."

My continued prayer is that God will be glorified
and that He will lead and guide me through this
process and not let me miss any lesson He's prepared
for me.

With much love and thankfulness,
Darlene

Practical suggestions for patients, family, and friends:

- Reach out and let the patient and family know that you are praying for him or her with cards.
- Offer to be the friend who will let others know what is happening with his or her health so he or she doesn't constantly have to communicate.
- Give specific prayer needs.

To the patient like me who doesn't feel comfortable allowing people to help:

- Do not steal others' blessings. God taught me much about pride and how to allow others to help—not only for me, but also for their reward.

"Two are better than one because they have a good return for their labor. For if either of them falls, the one will lift up his companion. But woe to the one who falls when there is not another to lift him up" (Ecclesiastes 4:9–10).

Chapter 8

In the Trenches

On June 1, my sister, Gay, flew in to stay with me. She's exactly one year and one day younger than me; we grew up almost like twins. Mop tells us we had our own language. I was the pleaser, and Gay was always in trouble—except the time I fed her dirt. For real.

All jokes aside, we were very close. When I started school, Gay was devastated. I was too, but I tried to be brave. I came home and taught her the ABCs and how to count to one hundred. She claims I was a goody-goody in high school and not any fun; I beg to differ. We have leaned on each other through good and bad times, like when her husband left her and her one-year-old, JD, or when her best friend died of cancer at the age of thirty-two. We're more than sisters; we are the closest of friends.

During that summer of 2004, Gay went on a hunt for a stage four survivor who could encourage me and all of our family. I contacted the Anderson Network, a cancer support group made of up more than 1,700 current and former patients. The idea is to match up patients and caregivers with other patients with a similar diagnosis to answer questions, provide support, and lesson the feelings of isolation that come with a cancer diagnosis. I remember how sad it was when they called and told me they could not a find a stage IV breast cancer survivor.

My heart sank, but I tried to laugh about it. I was on the phone with Gay when I told her, "I might need to read epitaphs at the cemetery." Gay did not think my attempt at humor was funny at all.

Gay became obsessed with finding a cure for my cancer. She says her business suffered as she spent most of her time searching the internet for treatments, joining chat rooms and forums for people with metastatic breast cancer. She copied page after page of research and was depressed to only find information on "palliative care." I answered her call one day later that summer, and she was noticeably excited. A woman who actually lived two doors down from her had been in her store and revealed that she was a thirty-three-year metastatic breast cancer survivor! Not only did her neighbor's story give me a little hope, but hearing Gay so encouraged also made me smile.

By the first weekend in June, a month had passed since my diagnosis. I'd experienced many of the expected physical side effects—nausea, insomnia, and hair loss—but some of the emotional side effects were beginning to kick in as well. I was taking Prednisone, a corticosteroid that helps with the prevention of inflammation and also helps with nausea experienced by chemo patients. But Prednisone is also notorious for its side effects— the round "moon face," an overall jitteriness, rapid weight gain, insomnia, anxiety, and depression. The initial rally hat and game face adrenaline I'd proudly exhibited for the first round of chemo waned as I sank deeper into the battle. The seventeen days we had to wait until starting the second round seemed to drag by.

Jay had flown in to stay with me over the weekend, and he was a rock—his usual steady self. All during the week, while Jay worked, I fought to appear strong at all times, as much as possible, for my parents, siblings, friends, and especially my children. For them, I tried to be on my best behavior. Friends would fly in, and I would think of the expense and trouble they'd gone to just to be with me and gather all the energy I had to entertain. I certainly didn't want to cry and make their time with me miserable and stressful.

When my daughters were with me, I tried to be as strong as possible. My parents were devastated, because for a long time, it looked as though the worst possible scenario for a parent was about to happen. I tried very hard to keep it together for them. Gay and I are very close, and she was in the trenches of battle with me. My battle with cancer had consumed her. I think if I'd cried in front of Gay, we would have had to take her to the hospital. The only person I allowed myself to be weak with was Jay.

But I was tired and teary that Friday and Saturday. Either my blood count had dropped or it was due to the crash after the Prednisone. I just wanted to feel some emotion from Jay, to know that he was hurting as bad as I was. Still, he was steady and calm, and it was not good.

Looking back, I know Jay was struggling to know what to do, what to say, how to help. He was afraid too. And I don't even know exactly what I wanted him to do—to cry with me over the situation or show more of his vulnerability. He did neither. He was the rock. Maybe it would have helped me to see his fright too, but ten years later, I still don't know. If I'd seen what Jay was really feeling, it may have weakened me. I just don't know.

For most of Friday and Saturday, I pushed him away and cried alone. I don't know what came over me. Maybe I was slipping into the "woe is me" place. Finally, I pulled up my bootstraps Sunday morning and decided to feel better. I told Jay how sorry I was, and we went back to First Baptist Church Houston and Beth Moore's class. And everything was good again—except I still had cancer.

Before you read this, you need a little background information regarding mannequins named Pierre and debutantes.

In 2004, on the occasion of my unmarried friend Irma's birthday, Jan and I conspired to give her a very unique present—her very own man. We gave her a mannequin and told her to put a remote in his hand, sit him in a living room chair, and voila—her very own man.

A debutante is a young lady who has reached the age of adulthood and is introduced to society at a formal party called the White and Gold Ball, also known as her debut. It's a fancy Southern affair with women in formal dresses and men in tuxedos. When Meredith turned twenty, she was a debutante, and of course our family attended the party in support of her. The Gore family was all decked out, and it was a lovely, sophisticated evening.

We sat with perfect posture in our formal wear at the ball as the debutantes were presented to society in their long white gloves at the side of their fathers in tailed tuxedos. We then ballroom danced to Motown and Mississippi Delta Blues music till all hours of the evening. Something, however, kept irritating the back of my neck, and I could not figure out what it was. Finally, after we got home late that night, I discovered I'd left a pink Velcro roller in the back of my hair. So much for sophistication.

On June 6, I knew Gay had to leave for home. I was a little down until my daily walk to the mailbox, when I opened a package with a video tape enclosed from home! Fifty of my closest friends got together and made me a chemo fight song. When the video first came on, they were all gathered in the beautiful, historical sanctuary of First United Methodist Church located in downtown Grenada. I was expecting something divinely inspirational when I noticed that everyone had a pink roller in his or her hair. And then I spotted Pierre in the front row with panties on!

My friends started singing a chemotherapy fight song they had written to the tune of the Ole Miss fight chant, "Forward Rebels." I cried all the way through it the first time to see so many wonderful friends trying to make me laugh. Gay and I watched it over and over and laughed a lot. I decided to share it with other cancer patients at the Rotary House on video night. My friends even made the big time, as CNN was filming a special at MDA and interviewed me along with other cancer patients. The crew loved the song and said it was a great example of small-town America. I didn't even try to explain Pierre and the pink roller!

Gay left, but Meredith flew in, and she was engaged! The date was set for the following spring, April 30, 2005, and it was wonderful to have a wedding to plan—something to focus on besides being sick. That was a good thing, because by June, my blood counts were getting low; I didn't feel well and had to avoid crowds. Fatigue was a daily battle, emotionally and physically. I was very grateful to be at such a wonderful cancer center but incredibly homesick. We'd left home more than a month before, and I started to forget what my own bed felt like!

Practical suggestions for friends and supporters:

- Gift certificates are wonderful gifts. My favorites were for things like massages, meals, and smoothies.
- Don't stop sending cards.
- Offer to take care of wedding gifts, etc. (small-town things).

- Keep in contact with patient's spouse and children. Send them cards or invite them over—whatever is needed.

"Let us hold fast the confession of our hope without wavering, for He who has promised is faithful" (Hebrews 10:23).

Chapter 9

A Mother's Love—Mop

I was reading. I lifted my hand to run it through my hair, and I noticed it—hair. As I took my daily shower, I started to notice more hair in the drain. There was more hair on my brush. But I'd remind myself, "It is just hair." I tried to be delicate with each brush stroke, but I knew it was only a matter of time before my head would be shaved.

In mid-June, Mop and Pop came to spend some time with me, and Mop did something incredible to support me. It was truly a sacrifice, but to understand what a sacrifice it was, first you have to have a better understanding of Mop. You haven't been properly introduced.

Mop is larger than life. She has always been and is beautiful. I think she could've been a star in Hollywood. She's hilarious and the last of what I call the true Southern Belles but without the ability to sugarcoat anything! She tells it like it is, and like any good southerner, she loves Elvis. She even met him once when we were living in Memphis. I was one and a half, and Gay was six months old.

It was the summer of 1955, and Mop was taking us to visit relatives when she walked past a mailbox that said Aaron Presley. Mop knew that was Elvis's father's name. She and two of her cousins started toward their driveway where, she claims, he was walking out the door and saw them. He started gyrating his hips, as he was famous for, signed autographs, and spoke sweetly to us babies before speeding off on his motorcycle.

Mop and Pop have a beautiful, elegant home, but Mop has reserved the garage for all her pictures of Red Skelton, Marilyn Monroe, and of course, Elvis. One of the pictures of him is even signed by Mop because she says she can write just like him. *Ha!*

She's also hung discs of her own recordings, "It's Only because I'm Lonely" and "Lock Me in Your Heart" in the garage. Yes, when all of us kids graduated high school and moved out, Mop went through a thing. I'm not sure if the term empty nest syndrome existed at that point in time. Other moms might have joined a club or taken up knitting, but Mop's way of coping was to cut a record in Nashville. After all, she says, "Honey, put on a big pair of sunglasses and a hat; walk like you mean it—that's all it takes to be famous!"

Mop has a way about her, carrying herself with poise and dignity, but at the same time always having more fun than most people dream. She always has a good, funny story to share, and if nothing hits her at the moment, she'll inadvertently comment on something that's sure to be a table topic for years to come.

Now you have a much better idea of the wonderful character who is my mother. I'm going to let Mop explain her unique way of supporting me in my battle with cancer.

> **Mop:** I knew I was going to do it. But I never told anybody—not Gay or even my husband, Sammie. Now I certainly did not want to do it because I'm

very vain. I just knew it was something I had to do. It was a God thing.

Gay had been out in Texas the week before, and when she came home, she said, "Mama, Darlene is going to lose her hair." That bothered me. Darlene always had pretty hair, lots prettier than mine, and so I thought, *Well ...*

We were leaving at noon that day, headed for Houston, so I said, "Sammie, take me by the beauty shop before we go. I need to get my nails done."

And I did need to get my nails done, but while I was in there, I asked my beautician if she had time to shave my head—because it doesn't take two minutes to shave someone's head!

She said, "Ohhhhhh, are you sure?"

And I said, "Yes! We are on our way to Texas, and Darlene is losing her hair this week. I don't think I can stand it if I have hair and she doesn't."

So she was the first person I told—my beautician. I took the baseball cap off that I had worn to the shop; she rolled me away from the mirror and shaved my head.

When I got ready to leave, I went out the back door because I wasn't ready to see other people yet, not ready to explain to my friends. I called Sammie and told him I was ready, to come and get me. I wouldn't even sit on the front steps; I sat on the side steps with my head down, still trying to avoid attention and questions.

But then I looked up, and out of the corner of my eye, I saw a car coming, just like ours. I thought, *Sammie is going to die—just die.*

With my head down, I jumped into the car. I didn't say anything. He didn't say anything. I just looked at the floorboard. There were new mats in the floor, so I looked up to say, "Where did you get these new mats?" And hey! It was a strange man driving a car just like ours, but it was new, and he was delivering the new car to one of the beauticians, and they were *all* standing in the window waiting on her new car to come.

I said, "You weren't in any shape to get in the car with a bald-headed woman this morning, were you?" He was just sitting there, not saying a word, so I jumped out of the car, and there was all those beauticians standing in the window looking. But they didn't know me without any hair. *Ha!*

Then I saw Sammie was pulling in behind, and I ran and jumped in his car. (He didn't even notice I'd been in the car with a strange man.) We drove all the way over to Gay's store, HoneyBaked Ham, to get food for the trip. We ran in to get the food, and Gay was in the back office. She saw and said, "Mama!" But I put my hand up for her just to be quiet because Sammie hadn't even noticed.

I went to the front of the store to pay for the food, and there was my youngest son, Max. He said, "Mama! What happened to your hair?"

I explained to him, and he immediately asked, "What did Dad say?"

I said, "He hasn't even noticed it. That's how much attention your daddy pays me!"

Now, I still had my baseball cap on, and when Sammie drives, he looks straight ahead. He really hadn't noticed me, but when he pulled up to the front door to get me, he saw a bunch of folks in the front, laughing and carrying on. Then he noticed—and he did not like it. He didn't understand.

He said, "Darlene is not a baby. She's not a little girl anymore. You didn't have to shave your head."

I said, "Look! I did it for me." And then we didn't speak most of the way to Houston.

And when we got to Darlene's, it was late, and she opened the door. She said, "Mama! Why did you do that?" She reacts just like her daddy.

I yelled, "I did it for me! Just hush!" So that was that. And I would do it again. It was a God thing.

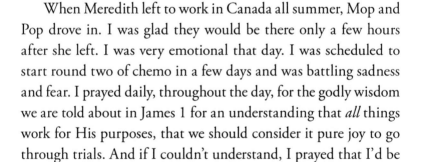

When Meredith left to work in Canada all summer, Mop and Pop drove in. I was glad they would be there only a few hours after she left. I was very emotional that day. I was scheduled to start round two of chemo in a few days and was battling sadness and fear. I prayed daily, throughout the day, for the godly wisdom we are told about in James 1 for an understanding that *all* things work for His purposes, that we should consider it pure joy to go through trials. And if I couldn't understand, I prayed that I'd be able to believe, have comfort, and know His plan is sovereign.

I was most vulnerable when I was alone. We had just moved me out of the Rotary House into an apartment two blocks from MD Anderson. It was actually really hard to leave that place. On some level, I knew I was here for the long haul, to fight this cancer. I hated leaving the warm and friendly people there, some of whom I'd gotten to know over the past month.

People come and go in the Rotary House, and it was a reminder that maybe I'd get to leave to go home soon. Either way, the apartment was nice. The two-bedroom unit was furnished with colorful, cheery furniture, as I'd requested. There was a balcony overlooking Hermann Park, a serene grassy area in the middle of downtown Houston that was walking distance from the quaint Rice Village, where my favorite restaurants and shops were located. But it wasn't home.

Pop and Mop drove up later that afternoon, and as I opened the door, I saw Mop reach for her hat. She didn't say anything but slung it off her head as if to say, "I'm here for you." I was angry at first; there was no need for her to do that. After a few moments, I realized she did it to help connect with what I was going through. It was truly a sweet thing to do. She and I both knew I'd have to shave my head that week.

"Strength and dignity are her clothing, and she smiles at the future. She opens her mouth in wisdom, and the teaching of kindness is on her tongue. Her children rise up and bless her" (Proverbs 31:25–26, 28).

Thank you, Mom.

Chapter 10

The Daily Battle

Be strong in the Lord, and in the strength of His might. Put on the full armor of God, that you may be able to stand firm against the schemes of the devil. For our struggle is not against flesh and blood, but against the rulers, against the powers, against the world forces of this darkness, against the spiritual forces of wickedness in the heavenly places. Therefore, take up the full armor of God, that you may be able to resist in the evil day, and having done everything, to stand firm.
—Ephesians 6:10–13

On June 10, I saw Dr. Esteva to check if my white counts were high enough to start the next round of chemo. I'd gained seven pounds, and he said the chemo might make me gain weight. But hey, it might have been the bread. When he examined me and said one tumor might be a little smaller, I almost jumped up to hug him. He quickly said it could have been due to the swelling from the biopsies. But the good news was that they hadn't grown!

Thankfully, my white blood count was back up to acceptable levels, so I was able to start round two of chemo that day. This time, I had more questions about nutrition and exercise, and he told me to stay away from soy products, as my cancer was estrogen-driven. He encouraged me to keep exercising, even while on the pump, as some research said it helps lesson side effects. I tried to be the most compliant patient he'd ever had, so I knew I better get to work!

Other patients shared some wonderfully helpful remedies and coping strategies with me. Cancerland is a community, and patients try to help each other out as much as possible. It may have been in the waiting room, walking through the sitting room, the butterfly garden at the Rotary House, or maybe even in the coffee line in the morning—the common ground we shared lent the way for easy conversations.

Much in the same way as pregnant women ask each other questions like "When are you due?" "Boy or girl?" or "What works for morning sickness?" the usual dialogue in Cancerland might go like this: "Where are you in your treatment?" "Just finished my fourth round … you?" "I was sick after round three and …" "What kind of cancer and what stage?" "What have been your worst side effects, and what works for you?" Some of the best advice I received was to keep a daily routine—to get up and get dressed every day, even when I didn't feel like it. What I consider as the most important thing someone told me was to develop my *own* routine. Here is what worked best for *me:*

- Each morning, the moment I opened my eyes, I looked out the window and said, 'Thank you, Lord, for this day. Please give me the strength to do what I need to do today." It was important for me to start out the day on a positive note with a spirit of gratitude. Many days, I sang, "This is the day, this is the day, that the Lord has made."

- I cut out all caffeine and dairy after reading of possible interactions with chemo and cancer. Instead of reaching for my morning cup of Joe, I reached for my Bible. I read Scriptures—a chapter from Psalms and a chapter from the New Testament—followed by a daily devotional from books like *Streams in the Desert* by L. B. Cowan, *God Calling* by A.J. Russell, or *My Utmost for His Highest* by Oswald Chambers. I also reread lessons from *Believing God* by Beth Moore. God gave me the wisdom to know that before my feet ever hit the floor, I needed to be armed with His Word. I never even missed the coffee.

- After getting out of bed, I would gargle with baking soda and water. There are a number of mouth problems that can be caused by chemo: sores in the mouth or throat, painful gums, and dry mouth. Chemo patients are advised not to use store- bought mouthwashes, as the alcohol might only irritate sores. So I mixed ½ teaspoon of baking soda with eight ounces of water. A fellow patient suggested I gargle four times a day, and this was very effective for the mouth sores, as was holding ice chips in my mouth during chemo. I began experiencing some very painful sores after the second round of chemo; that was when I began the baking soda ritual.

- I would take the medication necessary to deal with whatever chemo side effects I experienced at the time. For instance, I took the prescription drug Zofran to help with nausea, an OTC stool softener to avoid constipation, or Immodium if diarrhea was an issue and then Ambien at night to help me sleep. For me, sleep was a problem due to stress but was compounded due to the hyperactivity and jitteriness associated with chemo treatment. I was methodical about keeping a list of the medications I took and when I took them. It was necessary because there was a lot to remember (my nickname isn't DingDing for nothing!) but also because the timing of the drugs was important. I learned that it was best to take Zofran *before* nausea set in—for me, twenty-four hours in advance. It was much easier, I was told, to stay on top or ahead of the nausea; it was much harder to control once it started. Another patient suggested eating hard ginger candy to combat nausea, and it helped too.

- I would have a small breakfast, usually dry toast and an egg for protein. In general, I tried to be very careful about what I ate just prior to, during, and the week after chemo. Spicy foods made me feel sick during chemo, so I stuck to a bland diet. However, any kind of bread tasted just wonderful at any time. I was always ready to eat a piece of bread, which resulted in a thirty-pound weight gain. *Ha!*
- I would do breathing exercises and relaxation techniques that I learned at the Place of Wellness, a wonderful place at MD Anderson where oncology teams work with wellness staff members to tailor programs that best complement the patient's medical care. I went to classes about three times a week, trying anything that claimed to help with anxiety—visual imagery, relaxing (on command), and yoga.
- If at all possible, I worked out on a treadmill. The apartment I moved into had an exercise gym that I frequented. Exercise is a great combatant of fatigue, one of the most common side effects of chemo, and a natural mood booster.
- For lunch, I usually ate a sandwich of some type (my favorite was peanut butter) and fruit.

- Fresh air was, for me, a great combatant to fatigue, so I made an effort to get outside every afternoon, whether I had medical appointments or just took walks. After moving to the apartment, I walked to the mailbox, usually the highlight of my day, or across the street to a park with a beautiful rose garden.

- During the late afternoon, I read mostly humorous books, stories, or e-mails—anything light to distract my mind from the seriousness of cancer. I also completed crossword puzzles, anything to work my mind and stave off the chemo brain. I never really experienced significant problems with "chemo fog," as it's sometimes called. Some patients told me stories about struggling to find the right words in conversation. I just found that after about round three of the chemo in July, I wasn't thinking quite as clearly. When you're recovering from the flu or any illness, you're not as mentally sharp as usual. I do think it's as important for the brain to exercise as the body when going through treatment.

- For dinner, I tried to eat some type of protein, like chicken or fish, and veggies. And then I watched sitcoms on TV—anything funny like *Everybody Loves Raymond, Golden Girls, Cheers,* or *Seinfeld.* I steered clear of any movies that were sad or scary. I didn't want to trigger any emotions that were almost always barely below the surface. I simply wanted to end the day laughing.

By the middle of June, I'd completed two rounds of chemo with six more to go. Some days were difficult, but the next day was almost always better. The thing to remember, when you're in the middle of treatment and you feel badly, is that it will pass.

June 15 was the day my head was shaved. I made an appointment at a nearby store that sold real hair wigs to have my head shaved and then be fitted for a wig.

I prayed for the right perspective and tried to be positive. As crazy as it sounds, being bald was really a blessing, because it was almost impossible to wash my hair without getting the CVC dressing wet. And on all the days that I didn't even feel like fixing my hair, no problem. I wouldn't have any to fix!

Mop sat right in front of me calmly and confidently with her head already shaved, and it gave me strength to see her as they shaved mine. She couldn't take the chemo for me, although I knew she would have if she could have.

We ordered the wig that day too. They were able to look at what hair I had left and the picture of myself I'd brought along to match up hair color, style, etc. It was expensive, about $1,000, but fortunately Dr. Esteva wrote a prescription for a cranial prosthesis (which I found hilarious), and it was billed to my insurance. I would have never ordered a real hair wig had it not been for Meredith's upcoming wedding!

The wig was uncomfortable and the farthest thing from real hair that I could imagine. I remember thinking it looked like one of those Brillo pads I scrubbed my sink with. The texture was not natural, and after several attempts of styling, I gave up. It still looked atrocious, but I kept telling myself, *Looks don't matter.*

Mop and I walked around afterward, two baldies, and people didn't know who the patient was!

Suggestions for family and friends:

- Fatigue is difficult for most people undergoing treatment. Long phone calls and long visits are a problem.

For the patient:

- Choose to live. Be a fighter each and every day.

"I call heaven and earth to witness against you today, that I have set before you life and death, the blessing and the curse. So choose life in order that you may live, you and your descendants" (Deuteronomy 30:19).

Chapter 11

Reminiscing and Making New Memories— Even Now

I joked that getting ready in the mornings was much easier without frustrating bad hair days, but needless to say, I was self-conscious. It was as if I finally understood the peculiar little way Bogie, our family's miniature schnauzer, acted after having his hair shaved in the summer. I was not embarrassed, ashamed, or even an outcast; in Cancerland, it seems like everyone walks around, baring their bald heads to the world. But I felt violated, and as if the chemo side effects weren't enough, the person I now saw in the mirror left no room for denial. I was sick. Life would never be the same.

I wore a big floppy hat on top of my real hair wig to Beth Moore's Sunday school class the Sunday after my head was shaved. In the midst of this battle, her class was my reprieve. Like the rest in between rounds of a boxing match or a halftime pep talk by a basketball coach, being able to attend her class and sit under her teaching was not only refreshing each week, but also helped give me the momentum to go back into battle the next week. The members of that class and their prayer ministry provided a solid support system for me, embracing me each week and consistently encouraging and praying for me.

This particular Sunday, Jay and I entered the class quietly; being noticed or even talking were not what I felt like doing that day. I don't even remember what the lesson was on, only that Beth kept telling the class to stop "wigging out" over this, not to "wig out" over that. I cringed and sunk in my seat each time she said the phrase—as if my big hat didn't stand out. She must have said it a hundred times. After about thirty, I had to laugh. Naturally, the cringes were replaced with giggles as I looked at Jay every time I heard the phrase. We were very tickled. After the class was over, I moseyed on up in my big hat and told Beth about everything. We both laughed; she said she doesn't think she's ever used that expression before and has no idea where that came from. I still laugh thinking about it.

As the weeks passed, having no hair really didn't bother me that much. If nothing else, I knew the chemo was working! And they aren't lying when they say your hair will fall out. By early July, I was completely hair-free—no eyebrows, no eyelashes, not even hair on my legs to shave! I was low-maintenance!

In July 2004, as the United States sent more troops into the Middle East to fight the War on Terror, I couldn't help but make the analogy: I had been deployed to Houston to fight this war with cancer. The chemo fight song my friends sent me helped gear me up for each round of chemo. We watched it again before beginning the two-hour bolus for the third round. As my body became weaker with each round, the infusions became a little more intense. I chewed more ice chips, drank more water, tried to get good sleep—anything to help with the side effects.

Grace, Mop, and Pop were with me as we walked across the skywalk to the Rotary House with the fanny pack administering the red devil. We stopped to sit in the cozy TV room of the lobby for a short rest, and we met an elderly black lady in a wheelchair. Like many people there, she noticed the pack around my waist, but we didn't mention it in conversation; we just kept talking about our families and where we were from.

She interrupted me as I was telling her about Grenada and small-town Mississippi. She took her hand, worn with experience that just screams wisdom, and grabbed my hand. She told me to look at her hair. It flowed down to her back—grey, thick, curly, and absolutely beautiful. Of course, I asked her for her secret. She said, "Grease your bald head with castor oil every night, then put a night cap on to sleep; your hair will grow back so much better."

I gave her a hug and told her, "Thanks." I'm not telling you if I tried it or not.

July 8 was the third day of the third round of chemo. I felt very sick, but we wanted to celebrate Mop and Pop's fifty-second anniversary. They wouldn't go without me, so I tried to rally and make the best of it. Mop, Pop, Grace, and I went to the top floor of the Hyatt Regency Houston for dinner, to Spindletop, a glass-walled restaurant that makes one revolution every forty-five minutes. It's at the top of the twenty-fourth floor, so it's a pretty great 360-degree view of the city!

While we ordered our food and waited, Mop explained how she and Pop met on South Royal Street in Jackson, Tennessee in the summer of 1951. Pop was filthy after working with tar and gravel on the roads and had stopped to hitchhike home to Medon when Mop strolled by with an ice cream cone in each hand and a flirty smile. "Where you going, girl?" he asked her.

"Hoooooome," Mop still says with a luring tone.

Pop grew up as one of thirteen brothers and sisters working on a farm in rural West Tennessee. Everything he has in this life has come from years of sweat equity and good ol' hard work—what sometimes seems like a lost art these days. Mop talked about her lonely growing up years without brothers or sisters, floating between a few aunts as her mother lived a self-centered life doing her own thing. Mop never knew where she would be or whether she would be in school from one day to another. She desperately wanted brothers and sisters. She and Pop originally wanted six children, but four turned out to be enough!

"He never forgot me from that hot afternoon," Mop said. "But I made him call me three times before I agreed to go out on a date with him."

"I don't remember *three* times," Pop interjects. "She must have liked me okay, 'cause after a year, we slipped off to Corinth, Mississippi and got married."

"It was so silly; we were too young," Mop said. Pop was twenty and Mop was two days past seventeen. He was going to pharmacy school in Memphis, and she continued to live in Jackson until after a few weeks when they told their parents about the marriage. They then rented a one-room apartment in Memphis.

"In spite of living in one room and sharing a kitchen and bathroom with an older couple who owned the house, we got along pretty well." Pop added, "I worked part-time for the school, and Doris worked at Sears, so we were able to buy a chocolate nut sundae about every two weeks at a small drug store down the street—a big event for us. When I borrowed my brother's car and we passed fast food, Doris would say, 'Oh, Sammie, let's stop for a burger; that smells soooo good.'"

Mop interjected, "And you'd answer, 'I can drive up closer so you can smell it better.' We just didn't have any money to buy one."

They'd planned my birth to coincide with Pop's graduation from pharmacy school and never thought about pregnancy sickness. Luckily, Sears was only a block from their room. "Doris would leave at 6:00 a.m. to go to work, and after twenty or thirty minutes, I'd hear her running back in the house, headed for the bathroom. She had the sickness bad and had to quit work after three months. We moved into the government housing project, Lamar Terrace, where I walked to school and work but was never at home before midnight since I was having to work closing shifts at a drug store to buy groceries." Pop continued, "As dumb as it was, the timing was perfect. I graduated school on December 15, and Darlene was born the night of December 16."

"There were some strange people in the projects, so we never made many friends there. We moved to Jackson, Tennessee as soon as I graduated and got my first pharmacy job. Finally, we were doing a little better economically but still not out of debt. When Doris told me we were expecting another baby, I took another job with Walgreens since they paid a little better and we now had two babies to take care of."

"But we had to move," Mop explained, "back to Memphis, then Arkansas. But we had four children then!"

"After seven years with Walgreens, I decided that if I had to work that hard and stay late every night, I'd rather own my own store. I'd heard one was for sale in Halls, Tennessee, a town with about 1,500 people. I drew all of my retirement money and everything I had to buy that drug store."

Mop always smiles when talking about Halls. It was a great place with special memories. I guess any place becomes more special where your children grow up. Arnold's Drug Store would become the epicenter of our growing-up years. We lived across the street from the high school. As Mop said, "I would rather all you and your friends be at *my* house than somewhere else!"

We all were taught salesmanship early in life, working at the drug store in the summers. Mop laughed. "And Sammie made little signs for Darlene and Gay when they were ten and eleven that said 'Do you know that two-thirds of all people brush their teeth with a worn-out toothbrush?' and pinned it to them to walk on the street with a handful of toothbrushes!" I'm pretty sure we sold quite a few.

Pop became mayor of Halls, a position he would hold for fourteen years. He has always had a knack for business and worked wonders to help the little town flourish and prosper. Gay, Leo, Max, and myself all went to college before Pop decided to sell the drugstore. He and Mop moved to Jackson, Tennessee, where he began his retirement in a second career in restaurant franchises. Above all the success Mop and Pop have worked hard to attain, their marriage of almost sixty-two years now is a testament of true commitment, love tried and true through trials, highs and lows, made perfect by faith in Christ. They are more than examples to me; they're heroes.

There were lots of soul talks that night as Mop and Pop reminisced that were very good for all of us. On top of having so much life wisdom to impart, Mop and Pop are two of the funniest individuals I've ever met, even more hilarious when they are together. We all had a good time. There was also more humor at my expense. Midway through the meal, I went to the restroom, and when I came out, I could have sworn those jokers were hiding to play a trick on me. I walked around that room about five times before I found our table! I wonder how long they let a bald lady with a big fanny pack roam around before helping me. Everyone had a good laugh, and I'm blaming the incident on chemo and a revolving restaurant.

Fast-forward a few weeks. The middle of July was difficult; the nausea was terrible, worse than the previous rounds. The nurse said it was probably a virus, cumulative effects of chemo, or something I ate. I didn't feel like eating much (except bread) or doing much of anything; I was very tired. I was thankful that

Grace was able to stay with me for most of the month of July, but our fun outings were pretty much nonexistent. My major goal was to stay healthy enough for my blood counts to recover enough in the seventeen off days to start another round of chemo.

We were on our way to the doctor's office to find out if I could continue chemo and were both very stressed. During that time, I was drinking about eighty ounces of water a day—just water, not coffee, soft drinks, or anything with caffeine because the doctors told me it's easy to get dehydrated during treatment. As they told me, plenty of water during chemotherapy helps to flush the chemicals through the body and ease the nausea. Well, of course, since I was drinking so much, I had to make lots of bathroom stops. But I was also worried about Grace. I didn't think she drank enough water, and she seemed to never use the restroom! I know—just like a momma. Well, we were in the bathroom, and I heard someone tinkling in the next stall. I said, "I am *soooo* proud of you." I was met with silence.

After a few seconds, an unfamiliar and confused women's voice said, "Thank you?"

Grace said, "Mom! That wasn't me. Let's get out of here!"

We laughed all the way to the doctor's office, and once again, humor set the tone for the day. And I was able to resume chemo.

Practical suggestions for patients, friends, and supporters:

- Patient: keep your sense of humor. Find something to laugh about.
- Friends: keep sending cards.
- Family: be available and encouraging.

"But we have this treasure in earthen vessels, that the surpassing greatness of the power may be of God and not of us" (2 Corinthians 4:7).

Chapter 12

I Want to Live

Is anyone among you sick? Let him call for the
elders of the church, and let them pray with him,
anointing him with oil in the name of the Lord.
—James 5:14

Cancer is an extremely personal battle. Yes, the entire family suffers and fights with the patient in many ways, but no one can take the treatments for the patient, manage his or her mind, or take away the temptation to fear. Only the patient, no matter how old or young, can choose how to think or approach the treatments. I fought the urge to sink into fear and sadness daily and decided the best thing I could do was fill my mind with nothing but truth, focusing on what I *know* through Scripture, not what we don't—my cancer and my outcome.

Every time I was in chemo, those two hours in the infusion room and most of the time on the pump, I would either listen to inspirational music or focus on the Scriptures in a book given to me by a man we met hastily in the Rotary House elevator named George Bennett the first week we were in Houston. Dodie

Osteen's book *Healed of Cancer* is the story of her journey with metastatic cancer of the liver and is centered around forty Bible verses pertaining to fighting cancer.

Maybe we had the look of newbies, like freshmen on a college campus. Maybe the look on our faces or postures told enough. George had a ministry of these little books—something he figured was a positive way to lift up folks. He told Jay, "My wife and I—we're leaving here, and everything is wonderful. We did not think it was going to be wonderful, and I just feel like I need to give you this book."

The book became so helpful to me that I wanted to get more copies so I could also share it with others. I called Lakewood Church to request more copies, and the receptionist said, "You do know about the service every Tuesday, don't you?"

Well, no. I'd not seen the service advertised anywhere, and quite frankly, I was skeptical. Just the words "healing service" called up images of those flamboyant, showy pastors on television who touch people on their foreheads, and the touched fall on the floor or are miraculously healed. I didn't want any part of anything like that, but at the same time, I was intrigued. Her book had been very helpful to George, me, and who knows how many more people. And she knew firsthand about battling end stage cancer. I was curious and just wanted to go see for myself. At that time, Grace was staying with me. I knew she would go to the service with me.

> **Grace**: Mom and I argued the entire way there because she refused to let me drive despite the fact that, due to her gigantic floppy hat, she had the visual ability of a dog wearing one of those cone things on its head. Needless to say, we were a bit tense as we merged in and out of a gazillion lanes of traffic, and I lectured her about how terrible it would be to die in a

car accident on the way to a prayer service for cancer healing.

We arrived late and pulled into the giant parking lot already full of cars. Mom parked the car and put on the mask and gloves required by her weak immune system. You'd think that with mask and gloves, she could have lost the floppy hat, but I suppose it did add a little flair to the outfit. We walked into a large ballroom with chairs filling the entire space, full of sick people of all ages. We could see way up front, where Dodie Osteen was individually praying with and over people. The service was in no way like one of those services I've seen on TV with people falling out on the floor and claiming healing. It was simply a group of people who needed prayer, and Dodie Osteen was praying with her whole heart in the name of Jesus. That is all.

We took our seats in the very back, quickly realizing we couldn't afford to expose Mom to all the germs for as long as it was going to take to wait our turn. We'd been waiting a while, and we both knew we weren't going to make it up for our turn before we would have to leave. I don't remember what I told that usher, but I wasn't going to stop telling him until he escorted us to the front row for our turn. We took our seats, and Mom and I linked our arms. I am not sure what I was expecting, but it certainly wasn't what was about to take place.

Dodie Osteen came over to us, smiling. She looked into Mom's eyes and asked why we had come.

Mom said, "I have stage four breast cancer, and *I want to live.*"

Just like that—straightforward, blunt. "I have stage four breast cancer, and I want to live." After almost three months, she knew without a doubt what she wanted.

Dodie asked, "What do you want to live *for?*"

Mom answered, "My prayer is to live long enough to see my daughter Meredith get married next April."

Dodie looked at me, assuming I was Meredith. I really think we all laughed when Mom told her that I was her *other* daughter and I didn't even have a boyfriend! She gave us a quizzical look, then said, "Don't you want to see *her* get married too?" At this point, I wasn't in the conversation anymore but was forever changed by what happened next.

Mom gave the most heartfelt "Yes" I have ever heard.

Then Dodie got eye level and face-to-face with Mom to ask her more quietly, "Well, don't you want to know your grandchildren?"

That's when Mom closed her eyes, clutching both of Dodie's hands, and from the deepest place in her heart, said, "Yes, yes, yes, yes, yes!"

Tears were streaming for both of us now. We had not allowed ourselves to ask for this much before now. It felt so impossible, so radical—outside the realm of possibility.

Dodie looked at her and then me and said, "Well, that is what we are going to pray for, then." We held hands with her, the three of us, in a little circle. We were sitting, and Dodie was kind of standing or kneeling in front of us. I don't exactly remember the words of her prayer, but they were powerfully spoken with utmost confidence in the ability of God. I sat, and with every fiber of my being, without even words in my head, I prayed—maybe yearned is a better word—for God to answer these prayers. This time, words could not convey what I wanted to say to God, but I know I was pleading with my whole heart.

I don't remember every single word that Dodie Osteen prayed over us that day. Grace and I walked in the door of that service as skeptics, but there were no CDs or books to sell. People were simply sitting and waiting for their chance to pray with a fellow Christian. Grace was bold to talk to the usher who took us to the front. I would never sit here and claim that the service is why I don't have cancer anymore, but I do believe that God was there, and I believe the Holy Spirit was all around us and Dodie. I have no doubt that she is an anointed lady. But as believers, we are all anointed, and she was praying in the name of Jesus the same way any believer can pray, the way God tells us to pray and believe.

> **Grace**: Ephesians 3:20–21 has been at the top of my list of favorite Scriptures since then. "Now to Him who is able to to immeasurably more than we ask or imagine …" Immeasurably more. Dodie Osteen had the audacity to pray for immeasurably more than we had thought possible. Earthly facts were limiting our very human perspective. God's plans are better than we could ever dream up for ourselves.

Looking back, my prayers before that one had been far too short-sighted and a great underestimation of God's capability. This was a major life moment for me, and I think for Mom too. So often, I have caught myself going back to this experience in times of uncertainty to be reminded of just how sovereign God is. I can picture God leaning back and smiling at those prayers and saying, "Oh, you just wait. I'm going to show you immeasurably more. Their names are Silas, Avery, Eleanor, and Garnett, and they are going to absolutely adore their Mimi."

"Now it is God who makes both us and you stand firm in Christ. He anointed us, set His seal of ownership on us, and put His Spirit in our hearts as a deposit, guaranteeing what is to come" (2 Corinthians 1:21–22). We are all anointed with the Holy Spirit, and no matter what happens in this brief life on earth, we are guaranteed eternity with Christ Jesus. Nothing is too great or too much to take to the Lord in prayer.

"Now to Him who is able to do immeasurably more than all we ask or imagine, according to His power that is at work within us, to Him be glory in the church and in Christ Jesus throughout all generations, forever and ever!" (Ephesians 3:20–21)

Jay still explains to this day that George was an example of how a simple act of kindness can mean so much to people, to strangers. Never pass up the chance to be kind, and even think about possible chances in advance so you're prepared, like George was. It's not easy to reach out to people, particularly strangers. Even if you don't consider yourself a perceptive person or good at reaching out to others, you can still make a little difference when people really need it.

In the same manner that George reached out to us, we met another kind soul, Kyle, whom our entire family dubbed the apartment angel. Kyle, a good-looking, twenty-seven-year-old with long blond hippie hair was beginning law school and lived on the floor above me. With a full schedule himself, including law school, he had many other things to worry about than some person with big hats who moved into one of the hundreds of units at his apartment complex. He met Grace one day at the apartment's swimming pool and then came by later that night to meet me.

Kyle was busy with his own life, but he was another who always seemed to be there when we needed someone. He was in the lobby, when we needed help with carrying groceries up the stairs; in the parking lot when we needed a suitcase carried; at the door, knocking when we needed a smile. Everyone who came to stay with me met him and was touched by his selflessness and kindness. Kyle reminded us of Christ's love and provision when it was otherwise hard to see.

Practical suggestions for patients, friends, and supporters:

- Be kind, and anticipate the needs of others.
- Do not be afraid of the person who is sick.

"Let him rely on My protection, Let him make peace with Me" (Isaiah 27:5).

Chapter 13

My Heart's Desire

I wanted to live more than anything—to see Meredith marry, Grace marry, and maybe one day, to see grandchildren. I wanted to live. Psalm 23 tells us, "The Lord is my Shepherd, I shall not want." I knew time was in God's hands and that He ultimately numbers our days on this earth. In reality, everyone must live his or her last days. After all, life is simply a blip of time in eternity. I prayed for understanding, wisdom, and courage to accept what was not known and what I was afraid was the likely outcome.

Throughout June and July, with such a poor prognosis, I did what the doctors wanted me to do, but I also began to quietly accept that my time was short. I thanked God repeatedly for my blessings—family and friends—and promised Him that even though I didn't want to die, it was okay. I also prayed for God to strengthen my family.

I prayed for Grace because her life has changed a great deal over the past couple of months, and then she had to worry about me on top of all the changes. I prayed for her to stay strong physically, mentally, and in her faith. I prayed that she would meet new people and feel comfortable in Oxford, that He would direct her and help her to clearly see His plans.

I prayed for and longed to help Meredith through all the transitions of the new year: moving, starting a new job, and planning a wedding. And I thanked Him for the sweet phone call from her future mother-in-law, during which she said Meredith's eyes are like her mother's eyes. It was very heartfelt and sweet.

I prayed for Jay, that God would comfort him and ease his enormous stress.

My biggest regret was that I would not see my grandchildren. It was a part of life that I had looked forward to, but I trusted God and knew He alone could see the whole picture. I never doubted there was a purpose in my battle.

"Not only so, but we also glory in our sufferings, because we know that suffering produces perseverance; perseverance, character; and character, hope. And hope does not put us to shame, because God's love has been poured out into our hearts through the Holy Spirit, who has been given to us" (Romans 5:3–5). The hard part is admitting that not all purposes are the way we plan or want them.

During the summer of treatments, I began to grasp what it meant to "Be still, and know that I am God." Anyone who knows me knows that it's difficult for me to be still. And I love to pressure wash. I'll even go to other people's houses and pressure wash! I'm not an obsessive house cleaner, but I love to turn that pressure washer on the driveway, porches, and house to clean out the scum, some of which you can't even see until you begin. It's amazing how much better things look when you get down to this kind of deep cleaning rather than just skimming the surface with a water hose.

I also love the sound of pressure washing. You can't hear anything but the sound of the machine. It takes your total focus, and you're not tempted to do anything else at the same time or be distracted by the phone, TV, or computer. You can't even talk to others while you're doing it. It's just you and the pressure washer. The cancer battle was just me and God.

No one could take the treatments for me or undergo the testing. Instead of fearing the stillness and silence, I grew to love it. I could feel a growing depth in my soul and knew that the Bible tells us that character is shaped most through difficulties in our lives.

Society tends to glorify fashion, makeup, trends, and tummy tucks, and there's nothing wrong with those things, but it's what's inside that our precious Lord looks at. Show me someone who lives a carefree life with no problems, trials, or dark nights, and I think you'll see a person who is not capable of understanding others who have been through sufferings—or all of his or her blessings.

Only after I began to acknowledge the likely end of this battle did I begin to experience growth. Never in my life have I felt the closeness of God as I did during that time of suffering. No doubt the inevitable stillness and reflection that I had time to do magnified that closeness, but my prayer is that I'll be able to say that I have never been more fruitful than after coming through this time. You can struggle against the pain or accept it, knowing that God is doing a mighty work in you. We didn't know any of the answers to the "why" questions, and I began to ask "what" instead. "What, Lord? What do you want me to do? What are you trying to teach me?"

Still, I knew in my heart that God sends the rain on the just and the unjust, but we, as His children, need to embrace His ways even when we don't understand what's going on. We have the opportunity to exercise our faith to the fullest in these times, to walk the talk. When we realize this, the rain that changes plans feels cool and refreshing. That rain is sent straight from heaven and helps us to grow and gives us a true joy from deep in the soul.

Satan loves to trap our minds in times of trouble and overcome us with fear and anxiety. God can help us to see that all of this is just a blip when seeing eternity—"A mere mist that soon vanishes" (James 1). The Lord was there, working through the doctors to heal me from the terrible disease. Actually, sometimes when I felt I couldn't pray, it was as if He had wrapped me in His arms. Lying flat on my back with arms spread out in my apartment bed, I would turn my eyes to look up and just lie there, basking in the power and strength of our Almighty God. He is sovereign over all things—good and bad things. He is with us in times of sickness, healing, happiness, and sadness.

I listened to "Be Still My Soul" by Kim Noblitt every day. Oh, how it calmed me.

Be still, my soul; be still, my soul.
Cease from the labor and the toil;
Refreshing springs and peace awaits.

Be still, my soul; God knows your way,
And He will guide for His name's sake.
Plunge in the river of His grace;
Rest in the arms of His embrace.

That same God who "cares for me" (1 Peter 5:7) loves me so much that He sent His only Son to die a cruel death on this earth so that I don't have to suffer. I can spend eternity (forever) with Him in heaven. All we have to do is believe that in our hearts (Romans 10:9). I repeated the five sentences from by Bible study: "God is who He says He is. God can do what He says He can do. I am who God says I am. I can do all things through Christ. God's Word is alive and active in me. I'm believing God."

I could recognize Him in the faces of the doctors and nurses, friends and family, and sometimes just in the lonely places only I would have to go. There is one thing I know: when you suffer, He will wrap you in His arms.

Please hear me. I do not say this to sound preachy, folksy, mystical, or even whimsical. Believe me, the temptation to give in to the threats of fear was present and increased daily. Every morning, from the moment I opened my eyes, staying in this state of mind was crucial, even if I was losing the battle.

July 28, 2004 was the first time I had battery of tests repeated to see if treatment was working—an MRI, CT scan, bone scan, and chest X-ray. From our understanding of the doctors' explanations, the best possible scenario was smaller tumors. I really wasn't even nervous at this point. We were at halftime of the game, and I was hoping for a pep talk.

We anxiously and intently listened to Dr. Estava. Praise God! The largest tumor had shrunk, and two others could not be found.

Practical suggestions for patients:

- Guard your mind to help fight fear and anxiety.
- Know that fear and anxiety are not from our Lord.
- Music can calm the soul. Make it part of your daily routine to listen to uplifting songs and reflect on the words.
- Stay away from negative people and media.
- To friends wanting to help: Help the children of the patient in life transitions. I will always be thankful for friends who helped Meredith in her move to Lexington and those who helped Grace move out of Charleston.

"For I know the plans that I have for you, declares the Lord, plans for welfare and not for calamity to give you a future and a hope" (Jeremiah 29:11).

Darlene and Jay on their three year anniversary (1980)

Meredith, Grace, and Moody family at the
Houston airport. August, 2004

With Dr. Esteva, mid treatment. October, 2004

Thanksgiving dinner at an Italian restaurant in Houston
with our "Apartment Angel," Kyle. November, 2004

Mop and Pop sharing in the celebration. December, 2004

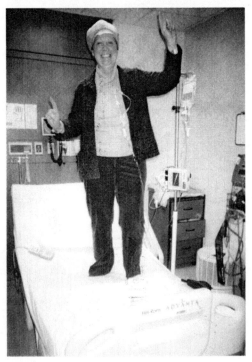

Celebrating! Last chemo treatment. December, 2004

Just before Jay walked Meredith down the
aisle to marry Bruce. April 30, 2005

With Dr. Perkins, mid treatment. March, 2005

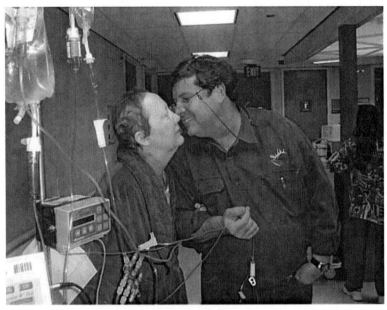

Sharing a thankful and happy kiss the day
after surgery. February, 2005

Bridal shower for Meredith in Grenada. March, 2005

As promised, dancing on the table at Meredith and
Bruce's wedding reception. April 30, 2005

Dancing with Jay at Meredith and Bruce's reception. April 30, 2005

My parents Doris and Sammie Arnold,
affectionately known as Mop and Pop.

Sharing a special moment before Grace's wedding. October 17, 2009.

Five year celebration of No Evidence of Disease (NED)! March, 2010

Blessings overflow! Mimi with her four grandchildren. August, 2013.

Mimi and Papaw with their four grandchildren. Easter, 2014.

Chapter 14

Homecoming

With a teensy bit more pep in my step and energy to fight, I began the fourth round of chemo. At least it was working. The doctors gave me permission to go home for the first time since May, and Grace and I flew home Tuesday, August 3—my first day off chemo. I simply could not wait to get home. Bruce and Meredith picked us up with my gloves, mask, and bald head shining. I rode in the passenger seat as Bruce drove us one hundred miles north to Grenada.

It was weird, going home. The familiar I55, exit 206, and buildings and shops of Grenada looked the same. Of course they did. As the vehicle carried us toward home, I couldn't help but feel a little removed. Everything had changed. Life would never be the same.

Still, I longed for *home*. I wanted to see dear friends who had so graciously and constantly supported me from home, who prayed for me daily and sent cards, calls, and hugs my way. We made the turn into the subdivision, and my breath was taken away.

It was a little bit of what I imagine heaven to be when we truly arrive *home*, with all our loved ones waiting to usher us in.

Two hundred friends lined both sides of the street with posters, waving and cheering for me. God certainly wraps us in His arms. Sometimes we feel it through friends who stand in the gap for us and truly pray us through. It was overwhelming. I cried.

Just before starting up the steep hill of our drive, there were more friends holding a huge sign with those five statements I'd held onto so tightly at MD Anderson.

God is who He says He is.
He can do what He says He can do.
I am who God says I am. I can do all things in Christ.
God's Word is alive and active in me.
I'm believing God.

I remember thinking that I understood how people who are disfigured or look strange in some way feel when no one can look at them without cringing and looking away. No one appeared horrified at my appearance, but I could see the reaction in some of my friends' eyes. I knew what I looked like, and I knew it was a shadow of the old Darlene. It was hard on my friends who'd not seen me since early May to see me in that state . Heck, it was hard for me to look in the mirror.

My doctors had warned me to avoid physical contact and strictly limit company due to the blood counts dropping after chemo, which made me susceptible to infections. Several people ran to the car and hugged me, and I just could not resist. But my close friends were the contact police and explained the situation.

Inside my house were a beautiful bouquet of roses, gifts, and food. I was overcome, as was our whole family, with the unexpected and unbelievable outpouring of love and encouragement. What a homecoming.

Being home for two weeks gave me the opportunity to meet Grace's new college roommates. She had already made the decision to transfer to Ole Miss from the College of Charleston before I was diagnosed, so we made the fifty-mile drive and enjoyed lunch with her new roomies. I wanted so much to help her move in and get settled, but at least now I knew she had sweet roommates. Driving through Oxford, around the square, on the campus from which Meredith had just graduated, I was taken back to my own college days. The fun afternoons in the Grove, delicious meals at the Pi Phi House where Jay was a houseboy, parties on fraternity row, and of course, football games—good times.

Jay and I didn't date at Ole Miss. I pretty much dated someone else exclusively all the way through college, and Jay was also in a serious relationship for about two years. Jay was a houseboy at my sorority house and waited tables, which was kind of an honor for guys to do then; the boys got all their meals free and got to be around girls all the time. And Jay probably dated every girl in the sorority. *Ha!* We were always drawn to each other as friends, not romantically. We just enjoyed each other's company and getting into long, deep conversations. We still do.

Although Dr. Esteva warned us about travel, contact, and infection risks, I was determined to make the nine-hour drive to Lexington, Kentucky to meet Bruce's parents for the first time. And, of course, I wanted to see where Meredith was moving, working, and starting her adult life. I had never been to Lexington but always heard it was beautiful.

The drive wasn't too bad; I was getting better at being still. Everyone was right—the rolling hills of the greenest grass I've ever seen (it's not blue grass, by the way, if you've never been) were lined with white fences are just like you see in the movies. It was beautiful. The highways are nestled along historic horse farms with barns more valuable than most houses. We made the turn into Lexington from Versailles and passed Keenland, Lexington's version of the Grove. I wanted to go there one day.

I couldn't wait to meet the Warfs, Meredith's future in-laws. I had prayed for these people and Bruce for many years without knowing their names. The most fulfilling reward as a parent might be knowing that your children are happy, safe, and loved. Bruce was everything I'd prayed for. I just knew his parents must be as well.

As we pulled into the restaurant parking lot, I was a little nervous. Here I was, with my Brillo pad wig taped on, face swollen from the steroids. Would they like us, a couple of backwoods Mississippians? Bruce was their only child, and if we felt that protective about our children, they must be just as protective of their son. Everyone was in the parking lot waiting for us as we pulled in. I hopped out of the car and immediately greeted them with hugs—Kay first and then Larry. They seemed very sweet and warm, welcoming us to their home as we hugged.

All was great until I leaned back from hugging Larry and felt a tug on my scalp. Then I felt another tug and then a draft. My wig was coming off! I caught it at the back of my neck and pressed it back down in place as best I could without a mirror. We rolled in laughter. So much for sophistication—again.

You know women and pictures. Scheduling a family picture was a yearly battle: me versus family. Many years, especially as the girls were teenagers, I lost. But this time, I scheduled our picture with no opposition. No one said it out loud, but I know they were thinking what I was: *This could quite possibly be the last family picture with me included.* It was a beautiful afternoon, and the pictures turned out wonderfully. Of course, I never like pictures of myself, but at least my wig didn't look as bad as I'd remembered from the mirror. Our favorite was the one of us holding hands and walking beside the small lake at our house. It's still framed in our home today. The photographer was also going to be at Meredith's wedding, and he took her engagement pictures that day as well.

The time neared for me to return to Houston, and I was emotional. I knew returning for treatment was inevitable, but being home felt very good. The comfort of my own house and bed and of course having my whole family with me was like chicken soup for the soul. As Sunday came, I really wanted to go to church. We sat in the balcony, and I wore my gloves, mask, and wig. I never went without my wig; I was no longer in Cancerland, and my bald head would have stood out. Again, it felt like coming home. The smiling friends—no, *family*—in our church were encouraging and further reminders of all my blessings.

Meredith and Grace didn't tell me they were singing that day. Grace sang, and Meredith played the piano, as they loved to do. I had never heard the song, but it was as if God was speaking directly to me through the words. The song was called "Gratitude" and described the overwhelming feeling coming from my heart that day and every day. Well spoken, Nicole Nordeman.

> So grant us peace, Jesus; grant us peace.
> Move our hearts to hear a single beat.
> Between alibis and enemies tonight—
> Or maybe not, not today.
> Peace might be another world away. And if that's the case,
> We'll give thanks to You with gratitude
> For lessons learned in how to trust in You,
> That we are blessed beyond what we could
> ever dream, in abundance or in need.
> And if You never grant us peace—
> But Jesus, would You please?

Being home was great, but in a strange way, it brought the reality of my battle to the forefront. As long as I was at MD

Anderson, I was surrounded by many other patients who were just like me, fighting the same battle. And while I was at MD Anderson, I was focused on the battle at hand, doing whatever I needed to do to survive. But when I got home, I desperately wanted my old life back. I was out of the bubble and wanted to feel good and carry on. For me, it was harder being sick at home.

Practical suggestions for patients, friends and supporters:

- Attitude – Guard your mind from anything negative or sad; fight depression with humor. Devote your thoughts to gratitude each day.
- Focus on the short term. Do not let your mind wander to the what-ifs.
- Trust God to give you the daily strength you need; trust that your medical team is prescribing the best treatment possible. (Once you make the decision on the treatment plan, trust them and do not stress about that plan)

To those wanting to help:

- Bring food that freezes in disposable containers. Label the containers with instructions.
- Pick up a grocery bag of staples (bread, juice, milk, toilet paper, paper towels, etc.) and drop it at the patient's door.

"Trust in the Lord with all your heart, and do not lean on your own understanding. In all your ways acknowledge Him and He will make your paths straight" (Proverbs 3:5–6).

Chapter 15

Sometimes It's Complicated

On August 23, Meredith and I flew back to Houston. She was going to stay with me for about a month before moving to Kentucky. Everything was going smoothly until I woke in the middle of the night with trouble breathing. Meredith was scared. I was terrified. She rushed me to the emergency room at MD Anderson, and three hours later, we found out the diagnosis was a pulmonary embolism, the official term for a blood clot in my lungs.

The ER doctor said, "You are fortunate. Usually we find these in autopsies." Well, that really cheered us up. I started daily shots to thin my blood for two weeks, then went on Coumadin for six months to dissolve the clot. I lost my beloved blue bracelet in the ER that night, but it was okay.

Resuming my daily regimen wasn't as hard after a few days (minus the pulmonary embolism, of course). Meredith and I were busy planning the wedding, and I was more than thankful to be able to do this, even though being long-distance made some things difficult. I couldn't bear the thought of not being here for this—for her.

We found an exquisite dress for Meredith. She's never been a shopper. Grace is my shopper. I think we had more fights when Meredith was little over her clothes than anything else! She just does not like trying on clothes or picking them out. We went into what seemed like every wedding dress shop in Houston over a span of a few weeks and ended up going with the first one she tried on. It was perfect. It was *her*—strapless, silk, simple yet with beautiful detail along the side, and in her words, "not too poufy." It was perfect.

Her good friend, Jenny Lynn, came to stay one weekend. She was more than a friend; she was a rock for Meredith during this year. In preparing this book, I asked for her thoughts. I must share them in her own words.

> **Jenny Lynn:** I transferred to Ole Miss my junior year of college, and Meredith was one of the first friends that I made when I arrived in Oxford. I met the rest of the Gore family that fall of 2002 when Meredith invited me to take the forty-five minute weekend road trip from Oxford to Grenada. I immediately loved Mr. Jay and Mrs. Darlene and so appreciated their willingness to treat me as one of their own. They assured me that I'd always have a home away from home since my hometown of Columbus, Georgia was a six-hour drive from Oxford.
>
> Mrs. Darlene, who I have affectionately refer to as my Mississippi momma, is one of the strongest individuals I know.
>
> The best support a friend can give someone whose loved one is battling a devastating illness is simply

to be present. It's not as much about what you say or don't say as it is simply being available and committing to being available for the duration, regardless of what takes place. There is an expression that certainly rings true in this type of circumstance: People aren't interested in how much you know until they know how much you care.

The true test of the depth of a relationship comes through the demonstration of commitment one has toward another when [he or she faces] devastating circumstances. I knew that it was vital to create a safe place for Meredith to process her emotions and to vent her frustrations. This was not about me; it was about her. Although I had to walk through my own process as well, I needed to remain focused on making sure Meredith had a safe place to find refuge. I knew that I could not change her circumstances (as much as any good friend would like to), and I knew that I could not be responsible or protect her from others' lack of ability to be a safe place for her, but I could choose what I was going to provide for her through my friendship.

I remember very early after her mom's diagnosis that I committed to simply allowing Meredith to *be*. If she wanted/needed to cry, then we would cry; if she wanted/needed to laugh, then we would laugh. But I never pressured her to express an emotion or to not express an emotion on my behalf. Each person processes differently.

I don't remember Meredith being extremely emotional all of the time. She is fairly reserved regarding expressing emotions, so I tried to maintain a balance regarding my conversation with her. If she seemed to be overly withdrawn, I knew I had permission to ask her the hard questions. There were only a few times that she seemed to be a little manic and appeared to be trying to avoid reality. Again, I would lovingly reach beyond the façade and create a safe place for her to verbalize the reality of the pain she was feeling.

My encouragement to others that face similar circumstances would be as follows:

- Be present, and commit to being present through the duration of the illness.
- Create a safe place for the expression of emotions.
- Do not force or deny individuals the opportunity to express emotions so that it makes you feel better; simply create that safe place for them and allow them the time they need to process.
- Do not add your own emotions of the situation to their burden. In my situation, I loved and cared deeply for Mrs. Darlene as well. Meredith and I discussed how I was processing, but I allowed her to initiate those conversations. I never offered/placed my feelings on her. I processed my emotions with others around me [who] were a part of my support structure.
- Mourn with those who mourn, and rejoice with those who rejoice.
- Be an encourager. More than anything, be a bright light in their days.
- Pray and intercede for your friend. It is vital to remain connected in the Spirit to have

revelation regarding what you should do and
say in the natural.

Jenny Lynn continually ministered to Meredith and me
through consistent encouragement. She would call and leave me
messages, simply letting Meredith know that she was thinking
about her and praying for her and me. Meredith explained that
she didn't offer any false hope or promises that she knew weren't
promised in Scripture. Jenny Lynn just listened. When they lay
in the guest room twin beds one night in the apartment and
talked about how hard it was to think of Meredith's wedding day
without her mom, Jenny Lynn said, "Don't. If you have to do that,
you will." Today, when I try to be a friend to those going through
hard times, I always refer to the way she handled this. She was a
friend in the right way.

Practical suggestions for friends and supporters:

- Be a friend who listens.
- Do not make it about yourself.
- Pray boldly.

Chapter 16

Joying Is a Verb

Weeping may remain for the night but
rejoicing comes in the morning.
—Psalm 30:5

October 1, 2004 was my twenty-seventh anniversary with Jay. Over those years, we went from celebrating with weekend getaways to just a nice meal to waving with a smile as we passed each other to and from softball tournaments or basketball games. I never dreamed we would spend year twenty-seven in a waiting room at MD Anderson going from testing machine to machine. I toasted to us with the second radioactive barium drink I had that day, and we both laughed. As Dr. Seuss says, "Oh, the places you'll go."

Music played a tremendous role in helping me to focus on God and my faith each day, especially during those long ten-hour days in cold machines. During one of the tests that day, I just couldn't help myself. Maybe I was having more trouble focusing than at other times; I don't remember. Maybe I was a little loopy from the barium. I can't sing a lick, but I sang anyway—loud. "Praise

God from whom all blessings flow …" One of the radiology techs walked in the room and said, "Praise God!" I knew then my situation was looking up.

At that time, I opened my e-mail inbox first thing that morning to an e-mail from Bruce, my future son-in-law. The e-mail was a powerful prayer that included a statement that sent me to my knees. "I pray for what we call a miracle, but to You it's as simple as breathing."

Wow. This was very true, and it was humbling yet comforting to know my life was in His hands. I kept singing all day, mostly to keep the thoughts of fear from creeping into my mind. As long as I was singing and concentrating on positive things, I was able to keep going. I tried to be strong, but I knew these tests, more than anything, determined my long-term outcome. By long-term, we meant a whole year. After hearing statistics, we never dreamed of anything more.

As I closed my eyes that night, I begged God for time. On one side, my brain told me to lie there and enjoy every second I had left on this earth. On the other side, I kept saying those words over again in my mind: "but to You it's as simple as breathing." As I took a deep breath, I recited words from Ephesians 3: "To Him who is able to do immeasurably more than all we ask or imagine …" and continued to pray through Scripture for healing.

On October 2, I awoke to the sound of what I think was God's whisper. I've never audibly heard God like that before, but it was His whisper. "The time for rejoicing is near." I only told Jay, my sister, my girls, and my parents about it, and it happened again on October 3. "The time for rejoicing is near." I don't know who actually believed me, but I clung to those words over the next seventy-two hours while we waited for the test results.

Tuesdays are Dr. Esteva's day in the clinic, and Tuesday, October 5 was no different than others. The waiting room was brimming with people of all backgrounds from all over the world, but all are the same in the world of Cancerland. *Headline News* was on the television, but that day, I couldn't care less. Anxiety was closing in with stealth, and I felt the urge to sing again. I think Jay must have elbowed me, because I kept quiet this time.

When my name was called, we went back into the same exam room we were in on that Friday in May. When we heard a light knock on the door, we expected to see the nurse come in for the subjective exam. But it was Dr. Esteva this time, wearing a big smile. He told me I was in remission and could go home on either Tamoxifin or Arimedex (oral medicines designed to keep hormone levels down after cancer) depending on hormone testing. I was still bare-chested and in my gown but jumped up and hugged his neck! We cried with joy as he kept saying, "This is highly unusual."

I told him he had no idea how many people were praying for me. Prayer is very powerful! I called my parents and told Pop, 'The day of rejoicing is here!" He didn't say much at first; I think he was shocked but thrilled. I called Meredith and Grace. We were all very excited that I'd be going home soon!

Then I called my friend Jan on the phone, and like usual, we got tickled by something. I don't remember what it was, but I laughed so hard that I leaned forward, hit my forehead on pole, and almost knocked myself out. Jay and I laughed and cried tears of joy and celebrated at a nice restaurant that night with Jay's sister, Debra, and Kyle, the apartment angel.

This is truly when my circumstances began to turn around. I sent out an e-mail that said, "The Gore family is 'joying,'" and I began to pack to come home.

After the good news, I was very excited and had to concentrate to hear what Dr. Esteva was saying. He explained that remission meant the cancer was still there but inactive, and more than likely,

I would start back on chemo fairly soon. But I had a break and was very thankful.

As we wrapped up our questions, he also told me that before going home, he wanted me to see a liver surgeon who he said was somewhat of a cowboy. He had scheduled an appointment with Dr. Steven Curley for the next morning. I thought of it as an aside, nothing more than something to do with research.

After we returned to the apartment that afternoon, I did my own research on Dr. Curley. I had read that he was leading the way in innovative approaches to metastatic cancer—hence the nickname Cowboy! I couldn't sleep at all. First, I was so thankful and excited that I might have been able to run a marathon. Second, I was conflicted as to what the next step was: of course, I wanted to do *anything* that gave me more time, but as always, anything with higher rewards comes with higher risks. I didn't know what those were at this point.

One of the articles I read about this cowboy's treatment mentioned "curing metastatic cancer." I breezed over the words and tried not to allow my mind to even reread that phrase. Wasn't that impossible? "If you have faith, nothing shall be impossible for you" (Matthew 17:20).

Trying to resist the urge to be over-zealous and create false hope, we bravely met with Dr. Curley the next day. He was a very enthusiastic guy and seemed to think I was a good candidate for removing part of the liver, which would create a possibility that we never considered: going for the cure. *Cure* was a word we had not heard uttered in my case; in fact, it was a word we were told was not possible with stage four cancer. Jay and I were unsure of what to do and just wanted some time to pray for peace with a decision. I was also very much in the mindset of going home, and I *desperately* wanted to go home. Dr. Curley said the entire team would meet with me the next day. Jay left later that afternoon to finish the week working back in Mississippi.

By Thursday, October 7, the next day, I still couldn't make a decision about what to do, but God was at work in the events of this day (of course He was). The timing of *everything* was incredible.

I woke up and wanted to ask Dr. Esteva some questions. My sister-in-law, Debra, and I just walked into the breast cancer center and asked if Dr. Esteva was in. We knew he wasn't; Tuesdays were his clinic days. But something made me walk in and ask.

The receptionist returned to her desk and said Dr. Esteva was in; in fact, the entire team of eight doctors was there, reviewing cases. The team was *never* there on Thursday afternoons. But the receptionist said she wasn't sure if they could see me, so Debra and I were both put in a room to wait.

Dr. Esteva came in to see us, and I told him that Dr. Curley had said I was a great candidate for the surgery and that I should go for the cure. *Cure* was a word I had never been allowed to conceive. I told Dr. Esteva I was incredibly conflicted and torn about the decision. I was very ready to go home, but now I had the opportunity to go for the cure. Wasn't that what we'd all prayed for?

Dr. Esteva, I could tell, understood my struggle with this difficult decision. After a few moments, he told me to please wait, that the team would review all of my records. He asked if I'd mind being examined. No, not at all. At that point, I'd get naked for any doctor who wanted to look at me. *Ha!*

I took off my clothes, put on a gown, and Debra and I were so tense with the moment we couldn't even talk. All of a sudden, the room was full of doctors. There wasn't room for another person to stand! Debra said I just flipped the gown off my shoulders and said, "Look! Everybody look!"

One by one, the doctors examined me, and they all stood there talking among themselves. Dr. Esteva just stood back, watching them.

Tears began to form, and I blinked, trying to resist. I couldn't stop them from slipping out of my eyes. One young woman, a very petite radiologist, saw the tears streaming down my face. She grabbed my chin and turned my face to hers, saying, "This is *good* news! This is not bad news. This is good news. *Rare* news." I needed to hear this. Debra started to cry.

As quickly as they all came, the doctors all left the room. Dr. Esteva told me he'd be back to inform me of their decision but cautioned me that the team might not agree.

I cried and talked with Debra. We were on our knees, praying. I was very ready to get home but decided that if the decision was unanimous, I would go with it. If even one doctor of the fifteen disagreed, I would not consent to the surgery. We prayed for peace and wisdom to do the right thing.

Dr. Esteva came back in room. I had prayed for a question I could ask him because his opinion meant so much to me. He'd taken great care of me. And I thought, *I've got to have his approval. If he doesn't feel good about this, then I don't feel good about it.* I looked at him. He had his hand on my shoulder. "If I were your wife, would you ..."

Dr. Esteva told me it was going to be a lot to go through, and there were no guarantees. He could make no promises.

I asked again, "If I were your wife, would you want me to have this surgery?"

He knew how powerful his words were to me. Dr. Esteva said, "Yes, because it would give you more time." That's all he had to say.

The new plan of attack was five rounds of Taxotere, another intravenous chemo drug, to further reduce tumors, even though a PET scan showed no active cancer cells, then liver surgery and breast surgery set for the first of January. I wasn't sure which surgery would be done first. Then I would have radiation for six weeks and go home with hormone therapy, most likely for the rest of my life. (Remember that I was told in May that I was no longer a surgery candidate due to the metastases: why would surgery help if the cancer cells have been through your entire body?)

The day's events are a bit of a blur. The excitement was hard to reel in. This was the first really good news. Nervousness and excitement walked thin lines. I wondered, *Do we try out a new tightrope to get a bigger prize?* Was I being greedy with the unusual results of remission? I wanted to live without cancer.

It began to soak in that God was giving us more than what we understood. The showers of His grace and mercy were like waterfalls after a drought, and I was almost blinded by the blessings. The medical team was actually talking about a cure, which is a term rarely used in a cancer center. This is especially true in regard to metastatic cancer. I had received a true miracle. It would involve five more rounds of a different chemo, two surgeries, and six weeks of daily radiation. I would not be going home for a while but hoped to make it to Meredith's wedding!

Debra and I went back to the apartment and cried. We called Jay, who was cautiously encouraged but relieved at another option. That's when he wrote an e-mail addressed to all of our friends in Grenada who expected me to come home. My friends had been celebrating with me because I was coming home. I was in remission. They didn't realize that the remission promise was maybe only for a couple of months.

Subject	Darlene 10/7
From:	Jan Moody (moody5@network-one.com)
To:	Undisclosed-Recipient#:
Date:	Thursday, October 7, 2004 9:35 PM

To: All our dear friends and prayer warriors
From: Darlene, Jay, Meredith and Grace

Friends: you have all been so faithful and steadfast and God has heard our prayers and granted us a huge request. In HIS own fashion, he has given us even more than we originally understood. We want to share this with you as you all have been such an integral part of our journey and we need you to continue the battle with us.

Today Darlene met with a team of oncologists, surgeons, pharmacists and others who reviewed all her test reports. Their unanimous (it's very rare for a panel like this to be unanimous) consensus was that Darlene's response to her chemotherapy was so good that they believe more than remission may be possible!!!! Although the word 'cure' is rarely heard at a cancer center (and never when one enters with Stage IV breast cancer) this team actually believes that by being extremely aggressive, Darlene stands an excellent chance of achieving a CURE of her disease!!! This is nothing short of miraculous. This is more than just putting the cancer to sleep, it is getting rid of it altogether!!!

The process is very rigorous, but, until now, we weren't even a candidate for consideration. The course now is to begin a second round of chemotherapy using a different drug for four 'rounds' of 21 days, followed by liver surgery and then, six weeks later by mastectomy and finally radiation. These are very serious surgeries and will come at the end of an extra three months of chemo....but...the reward is that the follow up hormonal therapy will have the goal of cure, as opposed to managing the cancer.

We need your continued prayers now, as much as ever, and God deserves all the praise for demonstrating His grace.....please thank Him again for us.....if it is His will...Darlene will have gone from a very dismal prognosis to a complete cure!!!!

Please keep us in your prayers!! We thought we'd be coming home for Thanksgiving and Christmas, and now we know God has more in store....keep praying, keep praising, and know that we are humbled by your love and caring and in absolute awe of God's mercy. Thank you. There is nothing too big for God to do.......and He loves His children.

Darlene, Jay, Meredith, and Grace

This time, there was no delay. The next day, Friday, October 8, I began my first round of Taxotere, much the same as FAC. I was in the same infusion room, the same sweet nurses administered the bag of toxins, and I had the same central line in my chest. But this time, there was renewed momentum. The feelings of urgency could not have been stronger. When you have cancer, all you want is for it to be *gone* as quickly as possible.

The side effects were immediate after the first round and every one after that. Even though it only involved a couple of hours in the chemo room (whereas the FAC went on for three days and a trip back to the hospital for a final round), it was harder. It bothered my eyes some during the administration, making them burn. It almost felt like my eyeballs ached, a weird feeling. I also developed a nagging skin rash that continued throughout the rest of treatment. Nose bleeds were frequent, and my nails felt like they were coming off, which was wild. I felt like a prisoner of war to this cancer. But I still wanted to do whatever it took. I strapped my helmet on tightly and leaned in for the battle.

I continued to pray for unwavering faith. "The Lord is for me, I shall not fear. What shall man do to me?" (Psalm 118:6)

Chapter 17

November Homecoming

Rejoice always, pray continually, give thanks in all
circumstances; for this is God's will for you in Christ Jesus.
—1 Thessalonians 5:16–18

After seven rounds of intense chemotherapy, my body began to
feel the cumulative effect. My blood counts did not rebound as
quickly in between rounds. In my eyes, this was okay because I
knew it was working on the cancer. The Taxotere hit me hard, but
I was determined to keep going on with life. I didn't want to miss
anything, especially if this was the end for me. I truly believed I had
been given another chance but continued with a quiet acceptance
that I might have gained months, not necessarily years.

Grace's twenty-first birthday was in early November, and
I really wanted to go home again, even if just for a week. My
medical team had agreed to the short visit as long as I was mindful
of my weakened immune system and stayed away from crowds.

Jay and I took Grace and some of her friends to City Grocery,
a wonderful restaurant in Oxford on November 4, her birthday.
Twenty-one years. Had it really been that long since she was born?

It seemed like it was yesterday when she was running around with her dark brown ringlets bouncing on her head. Her preschool teacher had dubbed her "chatterbox," and we knew it was fitting for our little social butterfly. Grace has always been a talker, an imaginative, almost mischievous free spirit, walking to the beat of her own drum. She was only sixteen months younger than Meredith but could not be more different.

While Meredith might have sat listening to music, figuring out a puzzle, or looking at a book, Grace might make laps around the coffee table, singing her own song. We have actually rescued her from in between the back doors of our house when she locked her little four-year-old self there, her tiny nose smashed against the glass. I told her she really did look like a mannequin, as she was pretending to be. Oh, the stories. Meredith was the athlete, and Grace was the cheerleader. I've already mentioned that Meredith hated to shop (like her momma), but Grace has always been quite the fashionista with a knack for style, like Mop.

Grace had spent two years at the College of Charleston—her two-year beach vacation, as Jay called it—but was now quite focused on a career in audiology. I looked across the table at our absolutely brilliant and beautiful twenty-one-year-old daughter and couldn't be more proud of her.

We all had a great time, and I was fine. Besides being a little tired after a late night, which would have been the case with cancer or not, I was fine.

But the next day, I was at a local store when I felt faint. I drove the five minutes home, called Jay, and he rushed me to the emergency room at the hospital in town. He had arranged with a local physician to admit me on an expedited basis if anything came up during my time at home. My temperature had spiked to 104 degrees, and I was placed in reverse isolation, where the few people allowed in the room had to suit up in a sterile gown and mask to enter. We knew the hospital folks, since Jay was the attorney for the hospital and I had worked five years as the Director of Outpatient Services back in the nineties. They didn't say it, but they thought I wouldn't live to leave. It was Neutropenic fever.

Patients receiving chemo are at particular risk of developing neutropenic fevers. It happens when white blood cells, specifically the neutrophil population, become dangerously low. Neutrophils are important in fighting bacterial infections and act as one of the body's important defense mechanisms. Without the adequate numbers of neutrophils, the body can be quickly overwhelmed by a bacterial infection, which is one of the reasons that blood counts are followed so closely when undergoing chemotherapy.

Traditional chemo works by killing cancer cells, but chemo can't tell the difference between cancer cells and healthy red and white blood cells. One of the most serious potential side effects of some types of chemo is a low white blood cell count, and the first sign of an infection may be a fever. Neutropenic fever may cause serious complications, including death, very quickly.

I went to what I call the *edge*, that fine cusp—the slim edge between life and death and the place where I believe our soul separates from the physical body and goes on to heaven. I don't want to sound mysterious, because to me that's not what faith is all about, but I know I was at death's door.

I was in isolation, in tremendous pain all over, and my head hurt so bad it felt like it was coming off. The lab work indicated that the end was near: my absolute neutrophil count was 500. Normal is from over 2,000 mm^3. The lab technicians kept coming up to my room during the day because they thought the numbers were wrong. My immune system was simply wiped out; that's why I was in isolation. The medical staff thought I needed to be in a bubble because my white blood counts were the lowest they could possibly be without me dying.

My dear friend, Jan, came to see me, wearing a gown and a mask. She was very afraid. I could tell. She had a hard time talking to me, and that was not her normal countenance. Heck, we've never had trouble talking; our husbands claim we could talk the paint off the wall! Throughout the entire battle, she'd always said, "Come on! Come on! Fight!" Jan and Jay even talked about getting a helicopter to fly me back to MD Anderson, but the doctor said I wasn't stable enough to be transferred anywhere.

The staff was about to take me to radiology for an MRI of my head that day because of the pain. My head hurt too badly to even think about being afraid. I thought, *If this it, then I just don't want it to last very long. I don't want to hang on while everyone suffers.* I just lay back and closed my eyes.

It sounds unreal, but in those moments, I could sense the presence of angels and the color white all around me. The air felt very cool, and there was a peace and a momentary lapse of pain. The staff had been unable to ease my pain, and I thought, *Oh, this is it.*

But then the staff came and got me for the MRI, and I was jolted back to reality—to the hospital room and my body. I remember thinking, *Oh, well; I guess I'm still here. Ha!*

The MRI was loud, and the pain was back. This time, I was very scared. That day, I thought, *Isn't it interesting that I am going to die at home in Grenada and not down in Houston? And that's a good thing; it's going to be a lot less trouble for everybody because I'm right here at home.* Is that not the funniest thing? Just like a woman.

The source of the head pain was never determined, and everyone feared the cancer had metastasized to the brain, including me. Thank God it had not. The MRI was clear. The pain subsided slowly over the next couple of days and was finally gone after three days. After consulting with the doctors at MD Anderson and receiving a Neulasta injection that would help by body make neutrophils, my white counts began to rebound. Finally, after a week in the hospital, the counts were back on the charts, and I flew back to Houston outfitted with gloves and a mask.

"Yet those who wait for the Lord will gain new strength, they will mount up with wings like eagles, they will run and not get tired, they will walk and not become weary" (Isaiah 40:31).

Chapter 18

Thanksgiving

The Taxotere rounds not only hit my body with a harder punch, but also were administered with only about ten days between rounds. I was a little nervous about the second round, but with the Neulasta a few days after, I thankfully avoided the fever. The fun outings in Houston had pretty much come to a close. I spent most days in the apartment, trying my best to adhere to my chemo schedule, and maybe had a few lunches a week in nearby Rice Village.

The plan was to have one last round of Taxotere on December 7 and repeat the battery of testing for the surgeries on January 7. The doctors had decided that if we agreed, they'd perform the breast and liver surgery at the same time. That way, I'd only be under anesthesia once, and risks for infections, although great, would be less than with two separate surgeries. Daily radiation would follow for six weeks, and if the tests remained clear, I'd be home for good with oral chemo for the rest of my life.

So Thanksgiving was spent in Texas. I couldn't go home because of the recent hospital scare in Grenada. But our apartment angel couldn't go home either! He had to stay in Houston and study for final exams, so Kyle, Jay, and I all went out for a nontraditional Thanksgiving meal together. We had Italian food. Noodles weren't the norm for any of us, but it was a sweet and memorable day. For Jay and me, holidays after children were special, as we began to know what it *really* means to be thankful. Holidays after cancer are even more than that. We were all truly thankful for our blessings—to be *alive* and together.

Meredith's first wedding party was the day after Thanksgiving. I was heartbroken not to be there. I could count the number of her basketball games, softball games, track meets, piano recitals, and every other kind of event that I've missed on one hand. And now I was missing her first wedding shower. Tempted to get a pity party going, I decided that her wedding was my goal. Mop went to her shower in my place. Again, I felt the urgency of the battle, as the wedding was quickly approaching.

As we were spending more time inside the apartment and away from infection risks, loneliness and isolation began to creep in. I tried to stay positive, especially as sweet friends and family came to visit, but physical and emotional exhaustion had set in. I continued my routine and sang "Be Still My Soul" and "Made Me Glad" every morning with hand motions that I choreographed all by myself.

A few weeks before, a friend of a friend who lived in Houston called me to have lunch. She brought a good friend of hers who was a nurse at MD Anderson. I told the nurse my problem in finding a stage four survivor, and she proceeded to tell me about Bonnie. Bonnie, she explained, was a stage four breast cancer survivor living in Hong Kong. *Living* was the key word! The nurse told me she'd contact Bonnie and try to arrange a time we could talk.

I enjoyed the privilege of talking to Bonnie in November. She was a great encouragement—very optimistic and alive and well. She had also undergone surgery but had to have some intermittent treatment that up until today (and hopefully much longer), I have not had to undergo.

Bonnie came to MD Anderson three times a year and was due to come back in February when I talked to her. We got together, and it was wonderful! She's a busy lady in the financial world, and although we planned to stay in touch, we did not. However, this whole scenario is what prompted me to get involved in the MD Anderson Network so that there would be someone available to talk to me, a stage four survivor. The Network always calls me and makes sure I'll be able to follow up. They give me the contact information, and I make the call. Currently, I'm following several patients. One is a thirty-one-year-old with a small child who has stage four breast cancer. Praise God; so far, she's doing well.

My last chemo (or so I thought) was Tuesday, December 7. Mop and Pop were with me, and what a celebration we had. Much to Jay's and my girls' embarrassment, I danced on the bed when it was over! I was very thankful but was starting to feel incredibly anxious about the surgery; it was a new fear and very intense. I had never had surgery or even anesthesia for anything before. I continued to beg God for peace, comfort, strength, and help in preparing me physically and mentally for this war I was fighting. As strange as it sounds, being away in Houston, so far removed from life as I left it seven months before, made everything seem like a crazy dream—a nightmare that I hoped would end soon.

The Christmas season was approaching, and I tried not to be sad. I wanted to be home for Christmas and prayed for the opportunity but knew my counts must be back up before I could even think about going into the airport. Shopping for each and every Christmas gift online wasn't so bad after all. All I had to do was click and pay, and the gifts were shipped to Grenada, where they'd be waiting, already wrapped! I still do almost all my shopping online to this day.

December 16, 2004 was my fifty-first birthday, and I'd probably never been so grateful to see another birthday roll around! I thanked God for my many blessing and for keeping me safe thus far. My good friends know my weakness: caramel cake. Not just any caramel cake, but one from Buck's One Stop in Calhoun City, Mississippi. About thirty minutes northeast of Grenada, off the beaten path, you'll find one of the rare true one-stops left in the South. It was a full-service station (now I think they've become self-service), and as you walk inside the old store, you're hit with the overwhelming and irresistible aroma of fresh homemade fried pies, chocolate fudge, and caramel cake. Did you hear the background music swell as I said *caramel cake?* Behind the pastry counter are two elderly ladies with aprons covered in flour who greet you with a warm welcome and smiles. And their caramel cake is simply the best in the world.

My wonderful friends decided this birthday deserved no less than a Buck's One Stop caramel cake. So they thoughtfully ordered one and mailed it to me! I opened the brown postage packaging and saw the plain white box. I knew immediately what was enclosed. At the same time, I was almost upset because I knew that moist, soft, perfect cake could not have made the postal trip without demise. I gingerly opened up the box and saw the cake in all its glory, safe and secure under a single layer of aluminum foil! Can't you hear the choir behind me?

I think I demolished half of the cake right then and there. Endorphins, right? Sugar increases endorphins, and I needed all the positive energy I could get. I might have felt sick for three days after that—oh, six pounds of pure sugar and butter—but what a birthday that was! Meredith was there that weekend and slyly rationed the remaining half (or eighth) of cake and allowed me one piece a day. I still laugh thinking about it.

Practical suggestions for patients:

- Seek out others who have been in your shoes. It is truly a hard thing to put yourself out there at a time when you're scared, sick, and upset, but there are others who know some of what you feel. Simply knowing they are alive and well provides encouragement to keep going when the going gets tough.

"In everything give thanks, for this is God's will for you in Christ Jesus" (1 Thessalonians 5:18).

Chapter 19

Christmas 2004

Have I not commanded you? Be strong and courageous.
Do not be afraid; do not be discouraged, for the Lord
your God will be with you wherever you go.
—Joshua 1:9

"Life is difficult." The opening words of M. Scott Peck's *The Road Less Traveled* ring true regardless of who you are, where you're going, or where you've been. When I read that book for high school English class, I had no idea what that statement would come to mean forty years later in my life.

As the holidays approached, I begged the doctors to let me return home, and they agreed. But the ninth round of chemo had knocked my counts really low again. It was Christmas Eve. Jay was in the kitchen cooking, Grace was doing some last-minute wrapping in the den, and Meredith was driving home from Kentucky in the snow. I knew I didn't feel well and went to lie down and try to rally for the candlelight service at church that night. The service is always a special family time for the four of us, and this Christmas Eve would certainly be no different with a new definition to the word "special."

I knew I had a fever and a headache. *No, not again*, I kept telling myself. Reluctantly, I took my temperature, and it had hit 104. I took Tylenol and waited an hour before taking my temperature again. After the hour, it was 104.2. We had to go directly and immediately to the hospital. We never made it to the service.

In a small town, on Christmas Eve, even getting blood drawn was an issue with a reduced staff due to the holidays. They tell me my white count was down to about 450, leaving me no defenses with which to fight any infection. I was admitted to spend Christmas Eve in the hospital. This was *not* the way I'd planned or hoped it would be.

A doctor and friend of mine at the local hospital, Dr. Tarsi, took care of me. She came to my hospital room on Christmas morning, bless her heart, and sat with me. She said, "Don't come home again."

And I said, "What?"

"I do *not* want you to die on my watch."

I was septic. It was MRSA (Methylcillin Resistant Staph Aureus), a serious bacterial infection. It originated from the central line site and had spread quickly throughout my body in my bloodstream. This is what we were warned of back when the port was inserted in May, eight months ago. "Be very careful, Mrs. Gore. More people undergoing cancer treatments die of infections during treatment than the actual cancer." I had been careful. Jay had been meticulous when changing the dressings. I did everything exactly like they said. I was overly protective. How did I get an infection?

Christmas Day was spent in the hospital, but I was finally able to go home that night with Home Health to attend to the IV administration of Vancomycin, a powerful antibiotic. We had an unbelievable amount of medical supplies, from syringes to swabs to IV hangers, and of course, central line dressing changes. The nurse had to restart the IV many times when the veins just closed up. Jay still explains, "That's the only time Darlene's been in the bed two weeks—and, incredibly, she survived."

Life is difficult. That was a difficult time. The septic infection was a major setback, and the surgery in January had to be postponed. That meant an additional round of chemo, because if another tumor popped up, I would've no longer been a surgery candidate.

If there was ever a time when I got truly depressed, that was it. My body was simply exhausted, and I was devastated by the knowledge that I'd have to have another round of chemo. After all, I'd already celebrated the end of chemo by dancing on the bed! I thought my body couldn't take it, that another round would kill me. I was also terrified that I'd not be able to attend Meredith's wedding. We were already pushing the envelope when the surgery was scheduled as planned, but with the setback, it was really iffy.

Spending two weeks in the bed with minimal human contact will exhaust you. That was the bottom. The loneliness was overwhelming, and I felt fear grip me again. These were days I had difficulty praying and looked once again at the baskets overflowing with cards. There were hundreds, and each one represented a prayer. I would look through them and realize how many were crying out to God for me. Once again, I received the gift of peace during the pain.

"Therefore, since we are surrounded by such a great cloud of witnesses, let us throw off everything that hinders and the sin that so easily entangles. And let us run with perseverance the race marked out for us, fixing our eyes on Jesus, the pioneer and perfecter of faith" (Hebrews 12:1–2a). When things get really

130

rough and you feel as if you can't pray, you need to concentrate on prayer warriors praying for you.

Our Christmas tradition has almost always been to travel to Tennessee to be with Mop and Pop and our entire family on Christmas afternoon. Instead, my parents came two days after Christmas, and we did our best to celebrate then. Jay's sister, Debra, and her husband and children had planned to spend a night with us; instead, they had to come by the hospital for a visit. It was a very sad time for me. We always have a family photo made with them, and that time, it had to be taken without me. I understood but, I was also afraid that this was the way it going to be from here on out, after cancer. I didn't want to leave my family.

It was sure not the Christmas we'd planned, but I made a commitment to dwell on the blessings. I wanted to live, but if I died after this next chemo round or during the surgery, I knew I would immediately be in the presence of the Lord.

"In the beginning was the Word, and the Word was with God, and the Word was God" (John 1:1).

Chapter 20

A New Year

By the middle of January 2005, my attitude had improved, and I was not nearly as depressed. I just knew that the surgery was postponed for a reason—time for the blood clot to be absorbed, a better time for the surgeons to be focused, time for me to exercise and be better prepared mentally as well as physically. I didn't know. It was a time of waiting. I waited for the end of January, for another round of extensive testing to see if I was still free of tumors and still a candidate for surgery.

On January 12, I was, at last, finished with chemo! After about a week of waiting for my blood counts to rebound, I spent my time in Houston, trying to work on wedding plans, trying not to focus on the paramount events ahead. Surgery was what I had wished for—to be a candidate so they could get the cancer *out.* Now I battled fear; there was something about the finality of the matter. This was my chance at a cure, an opportunity, a chance to come out of the valley and bring God glory for His provision, grace, and healing.

I clung to the many times in Scripture where God tells us to "fear not." I was anxious about the cancer coming back and not being a candidate for surgery, anxious that I might not live through the surgery, anxious about knowing the right thing to do—worried about many things. Did you know there are actually 366 verses in the Bible that tell us not to be afraid? That's one for every day of the year, including the leap year!

Wedding details came together. The invitation list was almost completed, the flowers were chosen, the caterer was lined up, the menu was finalized, the band was booked, and Meredith's dress had arrived. Only one thing needed to be done: the mother of the bride needed a dress. I'd told the others that I'd wear green so that Bruce's mom, Kay, and Mop could go ahead and shop for their dresses, but after going through several stores in Houston, there wasn't really anything that tickled my fancy. So I kept looking, secretly hoping I would make it there. I would be remiss if I didn't mention that I hate shopping for clothes for myself. I despise, abhor, and loathe it. Poor Meredith gets it honestly.

Those few weeks flew by as I focused on the wedding—anything to get my mind off the upcoming surgery. My morning chemo routine stayed the same, and I tried to exercise on the treadmill most days to help with my energy level. As the days passed, I found myself emotionally torn between anxiously awaiting the surgery and dreading the possible outcome.

This incredible, unheard of opportunity had presented itself to us, and while we felt like it was an irrefutable option, with greater reward come greater risks. I was worried about more than just being under anesthesia; this was a very risky surgery, and certainly so with someone who was septic just six weeks before. I trusted the brilliant minds that came up with the plan but continued to pray for God's wisdom and comfort as I trusted them with my life.

The first day of February was the twelve-hour testing day. After the PET, MRI, CT, bone scans, and chest X-ray, including a few vials of radioactive barium, all we had to do was wait to make sure the surgery could go on as scheduled on February 4, 2005.

I never heard my phone ring on February 2. When I saw the message sign on my cell phone, I quickly retrieved it, terrified that something was wrong with my girls or Jay. I just had that feeling. It was Dr. Esteva, saying that we needed to discuss the PET scan results. With my stomach in my throat, I paged him to call me back as I broke out into a sweat. I couldn't do anything while I waited on his call except sit and tell myself to breathe. Finally, fifteen minutes later, he answered my page and said the PET scan was all clear, and surgery was a go! He reminded me the medical team kept referring to my *highly* unusual case. Praise God for being unusual.

T minus one day.

"Let us hold fast the confession of our hope (faith), without wavering, for He who promises is faithful" (Hebrews 10:23).

Chapter 21

Surgery

The day before surgery, I was terrified. Honestly, I'd been strong going into the chemo treatments, really eager to destroy this cancer, but something about being put to sleep, losing conscious control of my mind, and being at the total mercy of the talented surgeons removing parts of my vital organs was difficult to imagine. It was hard to pray. I could not focus on anything but the fear, and that may be one reason there are so many "fear not" verses in the Bible: it is hardest to pray when you're afraid. I looked (okay, stared) once again at the baskets overflowing with cards. Each one represented a prayer. I looked through them and realized how many were crying out to God for me, which was a source of comfort, a tiny respite from the pain and fear.

On February 4, 2005, surgery day, I was scheduled for liver resection and radical mastectomy. Jay and I prayed together the night before and that morning, and I felt numb as we went to the hospital at the 5:00 a.m. check in. We all prayed before I went in for pre-op, and I wanted very badly to be on the other side of surgery. I tried to be in a state of prayer and thankfulness for making it this far, but after hearing all the risks and signing the papers of consent, I did not know if I would wake up or not.

After I climbed on the operating table, the anesthesiologist told me to start counting backwards from ten. His eyes were kind, and I smiled at him, thankful that he was so personable. I wanted to ask him if he had forgotten to shave but resisted the urge. The next thing I knew, I woke up with tubes everywhere and was as high as a kite! I was not in pain initially but was upset that no one was there. It took a long time for anyone to come to the room, and all kinds of things went through my mind. All I could think was that I must be covered in cancer and they had just closed me back up and nobody could face me yet.

I remember asking a nurse where everyone was. Finally, Gay showed up and said everything went well. Then everybody started coming in. They tell me I sang "Oh, Happy Day" into the pain pump button. I believed everybody when they told me the surgery was successful. I felt total joy.

I didn't even dread the pain and recovery to come because the surgery was over, and in my heart, I believed *it* was truly gone. The cancer was gone.

> **Meredith:** February 4, 2005: I flew out to be with Mom for the surgery, along with Dad, Pop, Mop, Gay, Leo, Jan and Terry, and Kyle, and our pastor from Grenada. We gathered in the pre-op area early that morning and prayed over Mom for the miracle of healing, for the steady hands of the brilliant surgeons, for God to be glorified. As she was taken back into surgery before 7:00 a.m., we hugged her, and I refused to think anything could happen except surgery success. Mom was extremely optimistic outwardly, so strong for all of us. A part of me realized this might be the last time I saw her. Talk about a long day. Finally,

late that afternoon, after nine hours in surgery, Mom was in recovery, cancer-free. We were all overwhelmed with humble awe. Of course, God was (and always is) faithful. This time, His answer was yes. I am confident the only way to feel the true thankfulness and joy we did that day was because of the deep valleys we'd been through.

Grace: I am ashamed to admit that I was not there to see Mom go into surgery. In fact, I was not planning to be there at all. It is astounding to me now, the way I suppressed emotions and reality and tried to convince myself that this wasn't as serious as it was. I had mastered the art of denial. Thankfully, I woke up midmorning on surgery day while sitting in a classroom at Ole Miss. Realizing the weight of what was happened miles away in Houston, I immediately got in my car, drove to Jackson, and got on the next flight to Houston. I pleaded with God for more time with my mom and yelled at myself for not handling things better. Thankfully, I arrived to the hospital with about an hour to spare before Mom came out of surgery.

Thank God that Mom came out of surgery. We walked into the recovery room, and there she was—still pretty out of it, but there in the flesh, breathing. It was good—wonderful news. You've never seen someone so happy to be alive and awake on this earth. Outsiders may have thought that singing into the morphine pump was just a byproduct of the medications. We all knew that's just Ding-Ding. And she's still here, making us smile. And to think, I almost missed these incredible moments because of my own lack of coping. I'd like to tell my sister now, "Why the heck did you not just drag my tail to Houston with you in the first place?" Somebody should've slapped me.

Mom was being transitioned to a room, and she didn't need the whole crowd in the room, so we all went out to celebrate. I don't remember where we went or much about the time together except that the room was full of such joy and gratitude for such a huge answered prayer. We toasted champagne and all signed our names on the cork. That cork still has a resting place on my parents' kitchen windowsill.

The pain was piercing after a day or two. The abdominal pain was so great that I never even noticed the mastectomy pain. I told people that it's kind of like having a toothache, but if you hit your toe with a hammer, you would no longer feel the toothache. Thank God for good meds.

As I looked at my body, it was hard to see anything but clear mutilation—first with the chemotherapy, then with a scalpel; my physical body was ripped to shreds. And emotionally, I still can't find the words to describe where I'd been. Somehow, though, after all that, I felt stronger. Through all the pain and nausea, deep down, I could feel a new person starting to wake up—one with a renewed passion for this life, for the things that really matter. Lying in that hospital bed in the wee morning hours, I couldn't keep from singing again, loudly, "Praise God from whom all blessings flow ..."

I knew healing would take lots of time. I know it was hard for Jay and the girls because there wasn't much they could do to speed up the process. We were all very thankful and quite humbled at NED (no evidence of disease). NED is what they call people when there is no evidence that the advanced stage cancer had ever been in their bodies. I call it healing. Glory to God.

Chapter 22

Radiating

After *resting* for three weeks after the surgery, gradually having the three drain tubes removed, and gradually getting around better, I began radiation. I called it insurance that *all* potential cancer cells were gone.

I spent most of those six weeks in Houston alone, as the radiation was not nearly as hard as the chemo. It was every day for thirty minutes and began as soon as I could hold up my arm for twenty minutes after surgery. The technicians formed a mold to cradle my arm above my head and make lines on my chest with markers, being very precise about the entire area they radiated. I was hurting during the first radiation from holding my arm up in the mold, but I was determined to start, and it did get easier. Everyone laughed each day when I yelled out, "Just don't hit my heart!" (I was being serious.)

The actual process was not painful, and I really did not feel a thing; I only had to lie there and be still with my arm above my head. The room was cold, and I was alone, but the music that was playing helped. I did have to sleep in a cotton t-shirt and avoid any contact with scratchy material. My skin started to look and feel a little like tissue paper after a week or two, as the radiation burned my skin badly. I really didn't mind, since I knew it was working. I used Aquaphor, a thick gel lotion, which seemed help a little.

Moving out of the apartment and back into the Rotary House was emotional. I have no idea why. Maybe it was due to the thought of being back in the Rotary House and all the feelings of helplessness and fear that I had the last time I was there; maybe it was simply me letting go of all the suppressed emotions of the last nine months. Going back was difficult, and I spent most of the six weeks alone. I did get to come home some weekends, but I looked like an alien with my hat, mask, compression sleeves, and gloves. Children were actually afraid of me on those plane trips, which hurt my heart. I've always had a way with children; they've always loved me. But to have them look at my face and then either turn to run away or point at me and talk to someone else was the norm.

The extreme fatigue was cumulative and hit around week four. Radiation is not nearly as tough to take as the chemo, but I was so tired that sometimes it was hard to put one foot in front of the other. Maybe part of that was due to the culmination of chemo, surgery, and the extreme emotional journey involved in a year of cancer treatment. This year was much more than the cancer, chemotherapy, surgery, radiation, wigs, and even celebrations. This was a time of spiritual renewal in Christ, growth in faith, and learning to truly *believe* the promises in Scripture for peace, comfort, and healing regardless of my earthly outcome. It was a time for me to truly realize more of what is important in this life and why I wanted to live.

I spent those several weeks in joyful anticipation of the wedding, which is a celebration and depiction of life with and in Christ. His commitment is to us through sickness and health.

April 3 was my last Sunday to attend Sunday school with Beth Moore. I was alone, running late, and I forgot my wig. After arguing with my better judgment, I gathered the guts to walk into the class. The lesson that day was about courage. Oh, how I needed to hear it before coming home and beginning life again. No doubt my friends and others would look and analyze how I chose to live my life *after* cancer. And in my mind, there are very few things that are scarier. The last thing I wanted to do was disappoint people at home. God had graciously given me another chance through an obvious miracle of physical healing. How was I going to boldly proclaim my faith and daily live to show others this incredible joy that can be found in Christ?

The thought of plunging back into life at home and work was daunting. I had spent almost an entire year focusing on fighting a war with cancer, deployed in a faraway land. On one hand, I could not wait to get home. On the other, I was afraid of getting back home and trying to live with the fear of my cancer returning—a likely probability. Courage was the exact word I needed to hear about that day—me and my shining bald head.

I visited with Beth after class was over, and I said, "Well, I finally flipped my wig!"

We laughed, and then I shared with her my story of the past year and the miracle. She fell to her knees, and we cried tears of joy and thanked God together for His mercy and grace.

During those last few days in Houston, taking the lesson on courage literally, I ran errands one afternoon without a hat. On this particular day, people just *stared* at me like I was really weird. After walking into several different stores and getting the same reactions from others, I became irritated because I thought, *Here I am in the cancer capital of world, and people are staring at* me!

Finally, after running another errand, I jumped back in the car, looked in the mirror to reapply lip gloss, and I saw why everyone had stared at me. I'd worn my sunglasses, but one of the lenses was missing! When I told Jay that night, he couldn't believe that *I* hadn't noticed it. Oh well, I hadn't changed too much through all this. I was still the same old me.

I am *not* a shopper, but before I got home, there was a very important purchase to make—my dress for the wedding. With only about a month before the wedding, friends kept telling me I had to find one. While out one afternoon, I stumbled upon a little shop run by two sisters. They greeted me with kind smiles and immediately saw the shape I was in—no hair, weak, radiation burns, and obviously desperate for a last-minute marvel—so they took over. They made me sit down and kept bringing dresses for me to view. They brought me a bright green skirt with a bustier and a jacket, all in silk. It was exquisite and exactly what I was looking for. As I went into the dressing room to try it on, I got tickled. There I was, never having worn a bustier, trying to figure out which was the front and which was the back. And I had a missing breast. The sweet ladies were able to come in and save the day with special alterations.

I called Jay from the store; it was more than I had planned to spend. Good ol', frugal, tight Jay never hesitated. He knew what the best answer was and how much I had agonized over finding a dress for the wedding. He quickly said, "Buy it," and I did! I e-mailed Meredith a picture, and she liked it, so it was done—all in two hours!

My last day of radiation was April 8, and the medical staff let me put my music in the speaker system. I brought the song I sang every day with hand motions, "Made Me Glad" by Hillsong. I lay on the mold to have the radiation, trying to be very still, and the music played. My eyes were closed, and I was sang those words from the center of my heart. At the chorus, I cracked my eyes and looked over at the glass, and the entire radiation department was rocking with me!

> I will bless the Lord forever,
> And I will trust Him at all times.
> He has delivered me from all fear,
> And He has set my feet upon a rock,
> And I will not be moved,
> And I'll say of the Lord,
>
> You are my shield,
> My strength, my portion, Deliverer,
> My shelter, strong tower
> My very present help in time of need.

At MD Anderson, when a patient finishes treatment, he or she can ring a big, loud bell that can be heard throughout the hospital. I had heard the bell for eleven months now and longed for my turn. On April 8 at noon, I proudly pulled the rope to ring the bell with Jay by my side, smiling and clapping. The peals of *ding* and *dong* reverberated throughout the hospital, and I can close my eyes today and hear them again. As the cheers from onlookers were muffled by my heart's overwhelming joy, I knew the ringing signified not the end of a nightmare, but the beginning of the rest of the story.

Then Jay and I headed home! Wow. What a year! This journey is not over, and it never will be.

Practical suggestions for patients and caregivers:

- Don't stop fighting the battle.
- Sing loudly (with hand motions)!
- Respect the patient's wish to have alone time.
- Don't stop sending cards.

"And without faith it is impossible to please Him, for he who comes to God must believe that He is, and that He is a rewarder of those who seek Him" (Hebrews 11:6).

Revive Your Spirit with Women of Faith

Sometimes we are reminded of who takes care of us and who is in charge of all the events of our lives. Sometimes God turns things completely upside down so that what is happening does not make sense at all! We are forced to cling to Him and rest in His peace that passes understanding. You may find yourself in the middle of circumstances that do not make sense to you. You may be surrounded by people and places that would never be your choice.

God may remind us that the battle is His, and the way He wins battles is often through people and events we would never think of, much less choose! Oddly enough, that knowledge takes the pressure off of me. I can quit striving, plotting, and worrying. I am not the star of the show; God is. That brings me outrageous peace.

Chapter 23

Home

April 30, 2005, was the day I had prayed to see. The day that had been my inspiration and a wonderful diversion from the battle with the big *C* was a time of incredible joy. I still cannot describe it. I tried to take in every moment, praying that my physical state would not in any way put a damper on the weekend.

The wedding was held at our church, First Baptist Church, Grenada, and the place was packed! The sanctuary was decorated with beautiful flowers and even more beautiful people. These were people who had stood by our family through thick and thin, prayed for us, and gone through the trenches with us—God-given friends.

The clouds had hung around all day, but as time came to start the ceremony—two minutes before the mothers were to be seated—the sun broke through the clouds. It was a beautiful night. I was determined to be strong. I was too happy to cry. Of course I made sure my wig was double-taped to my head in several places!

The bridal party gathered in the vestibule and got in line to be seated. Bruce's mom, Kay, was seated first. The doors opened, and Kay walked to her seat as the piano notes filled the room with a song that illustrated my heart. With my eyes closed and a beaming smile I could not hide, I prayed the lyrics by Andrae Crouch:

How can I say thanks for the things you have done for me,
Things so underserved yet You gave to prove Your love for me,
The voices of a million angels could not express my gratitude:
All that I am and ever hope to be—I owe it all to Thee.

It was then my turn to be seated. I held Jay's arm tightly and don't know if I've ever felt so full of gratitude and pure joy in my life. *We* had made it. God and I had made it to the wedding. I stepped out into the aisle, and the song continued to almost shout from my heart:

To God be the glory,
To God be the glory,
To God by the glory
For the things He has done!

My eyes met Mop's as I turned to sit in the pew in front of her. Her eyes were full of tears, and I just about lost it. I can't even imagine the fullness of her emotions as she watched her daughter endure and now overcome. I still imagine that having to go through this with a child is even worse than going through it yourself. As I looked around at everyone, all I could feel at that moment was thankfulness at actually being able to be there.

Once I sat down, I had to start some of the calming techniques I'd learned at MD Anderson, because I was *not* going to break down during the ceremony. I didn't want to impose on Bruce and Meredith's moment in any way or bring attention to myself. I stayed in the moment as much as possible but did have to visually go to the beach a few times to keep from crying about the pure joy of being there.

Meredith looked stunning in her dress as Jay escorted her to the altar. She truly was radiant as she walked down the aisle, and I couldn't help but thank God for her and the woman she'd become. There is nothing better than seeing your grown children happy. When our children make us proud, it must be a glimpse of how God must feel when we do something that pleases Him.

The ceremony was beautiful and focused on the Lord and His great love for us. Marriage, the covenant commitment to each other, is merely the world's best picture of what it will be like when we are united the Christ for eternity. As the pastors shared what it means to truly *love*, I slipped my hand slipped into Jay's. He my Prince Charming twenty-eight years before—even more so now. We may have a few more miles on us now and a few gray hairs—heck, I just wanted a few hairs! But now we truly know what it means to love in sickness and in health, in good times and in bad, until we are parted by death. I leaned my head on his shoulder and thanked God for my rock.

Meredith's friends sang "The Prayer" as Bruce and Meredith knelt on the prayer bench. In a lot of Southern weddings, a song is sung as a prayer while the couple getting married either lights a candle signifying unity or kneels in prayer. Bruce was not a seasoned Southern wedding veteran. I looked up during the song, and Bruce was praying at the bench. I had never seen a groom do that before. Later, he said, "That's just what I thought I was supposed to do." It was precious and sweet.

Meredith and Bruce said they wanted the wedding to be reverent and the reception to be fun—and fun it was. The azaleas bloomed everywhere at the historic Troy Plantation. About nine hundred people, including thirteen of my college friends (who didn't even know Meredith but came to celebrate with us) and people from many states away, celebrated as hard as we could. We danced the night away with the SoulSations from Memphis. Mop, Gay—everyone was dancing!

Jan had told Mop last summer that once it was all over with, "We are going to have a party and dance on the tables!" Well, after Meredith and Bruce left the reception, I went over to Jan and told her it was time. I don't think she knew at first what I meant, but we got on the tables and danced. Grace sang "I Will Survive" with the band, and we all danced on tables! I looked over at Pop and saw tears rolling down his cheeks. It was truly a special moment on many levels. And Grace caught the bouquet!

It was around midnight, which was late for me, and I was exhausted but unbelievably happy. Jay still wasn't home; he'd stayed to help clean things up after the reception. I was home alone, putting on my pajamas for a good night's rest in *my* bed. I'd washed my face and brushed my teeth and was working on the wig. Usually I'd just pry off a few pieces of the wig tape, and it'd come right off. I tried and tried to tug at it, but it was stuck! It hadn't budged during he celebration, dancing, and hugging. And now it wouldn't budge. I just had to sit there on my bed and laugh. Grace came in about an hour later, and together we pried (and giggled) it off.

What little peach fuzz I had growing in, we pulled completely out. We laughed until we cried.

I am thankful for two special friends, Jackie and Pattie, who were extraordinary in the roles of wedding planner and wedding decorator and coordinator. "The Lord has done great things for us and we are filled with joy" (Psalm 126:3).

Chapter 24

This Is Temporary!

The Lord is my shepherd; I shall not want. He maketh me
to lie down in green pastures; He leadeth me beside the still
waters. He restoreth my soul; He leadeth me in the paths of
righteousness for his name's sake. Yea, though I walk through
the valley of the shadow of death, I will fear no evil: for Thou
art with me; thy rod and thy staff they comfort me. Thou
preparest a table before me in the presence of mine enemies:
Thou anointest my head with oil, my cup runneth over.
Surely goodness and mercy shall follow me all the days of
my life: and I shall dwell in the house of the Lord forever.
—Psalm 23 (KJV)

After college graduation, the guy I dated through college and
I went our separate ways. The relationship did not work out.
Jay also graduated, moved to Grenada, Mississippi, and began
practicing law with his dad. I moved to Jackson, Tennessee and
began working at a speech and hearing center. Jay had been a
houseboy and served tables for years in my sorority house at Ole
Miss, but we had each dated other people. I thought our meeting

happened by chance but later came to find out my friend, Gail, and Jay had conjured up a means of us accidentally running into each other in Memphis. This time, Jay called and asked me out. I thought, *Gosh, we're just friends,* but I obviously went on that first date.

We've always been committed to the marriage. I attribute our years of success to Jay's proposal in May of 1977. We were upstairs in his mother's not-so-romantic laundry room. But I'll never forget Jay taking my hand after I said yes and saying, "Let's pray." And he prayed for the Lord to allow us to grow closer to each other and to Him because that was the way our marriage would work. I always go back to that, and I've shared that moment with Meredith and Grace—the message that love alone is not going to get you through. If God is not in your marriage, the days when you just want to walk out and say "Forget this" are more frequent, and you might actually do that.

Now, lest you think our relationship is perfect, please let me inform you that we are both firstborn children. I am the oldest of four siblings, and Jay is the older of two. According to everything that is said about birth order, marriages in which both partners are firstborn children are the most challenging. I dare say they are right! We're both extremely independent and kind of bossy, and each thinks he or she knows what's best.

Jay and I are also complete opposites. He's very serious, matter-of-fact, black-and-white. He's not a huge conversationalist. "If you've got something to say, just say it and be done!" Jay is also steady and even all the time. I'm more like a roller coaster. I get really excited or upset, very involved with other people and their lives. Jay has lots of friends, but he's still a bit of a loner, an outdoorsman who loves to hunt and fish. I left my home in Tennessee, family, and closest friends to move to the country of Mississippi, and I knew *nothing* of hunting.

For the remainder of this chapter, you're going to hear straight from Jay about our experience battling cancer, and in particular, his role as a caregiver. This is a very important chapter for me, because it was only afterward, when I was well, that I realized how much support the caregiver needs—and oftentimes doesn't get.

When I was at MD Anderson, I was incredibly fortunate to have family members and friends to come and stay with me. For them, I tried to be on my best behavior. Friends would fly in, and I thought of the expense and trouble they'd gone to just to be with me. I'd rally to try and entertain as much as I could. I certainly didn't want to cry and make their time with me miserable and stressful. When my daughters were with me, I couldn't break down in front of them, so I tried to be as strong as possible. My parents were devastated, because for a long time, it looked as though the worst possible scenario for a parent was about to happen. So I tried very hard to keep it together for them. The only person I allowed myself to be weak with was Jay.

Jay was home alone, continuing to work, maintaining our home, flying back and forth almost every weekend, and being *strong* for his family. For the most part, Jay and I talked every day and tried very hard to stay upbeat, but there were times when he got off the plane, and I was very tired of being strong. I'd cry and cry. And then on Sundays, when I knew he'd be leaving, there would be many more tears. He alone bore the brunt of my moments of weakness, fear, and desperation.

The above was Jay's life as he knew it for a year. Jay says that in the first few weeks after my diagnosis, he was in so much pain and was so mentally, emotionally, and physically tired that he couldn't even pray. Jay said he walked around muttering The Lord's Prayer under his breath; that was as close as he could get to actual praying.

I heard from hundreds of people every week via e-mails, phone calls, and cards. Those cards and messages of support were invaluable. The support was incredible, but Jay didn't get that support. Of course, he has many friends, and of course, they cared. Understandably, much of the focus is on the patient, but few people understand the role and stress of the caregiver. There were people who occasionally invited him over to eat dinner, but he got nothing compared to the support I received.

And now I'll turn it over to Jay as he shares insight our battle with cancer and our lives and relationship before, during, and after the big *C*.

As Darlene said, we did not start dating until we were out of college. We had been good friends but never dated.

When we did start seeing each other, I drove up to see her in Jackson, Tennessee on the weekends. I was drawn to Darlene and married her because I loved her carefree personality and fun versus my seriousness. She was—is—pretty, ambitious, and very intelligent. One of the qualities that first attracted me to Darlene was that she wasn't a dependent person; she could stand on her own two feet and wasn't needy. Though she did have expectations of her husband, she could go to the airport, buy her ticket, and get to her destination without me. Most importantly, she loves the Lord.

I have always had a long-term view of life and living and have understood that what you do today becomes factual history. It never can be changed, and so it follows you—for better or worse—for your lifetime. I once told a friend of mine that if he only dated pretty girls, he would never be in love with a homely one! Of course, pretty is in the eye of the beholder, but the same principles apply to core beliefs and character. You can't change a person, so don't become involved with someone thinking you can. You just can't.

Being a Christian carries many correlative traits that I believe are necessary for the level of commitment required to make a marriage work, especially in times of trial and tribulation—for us, cancer. The word *enduring* has two meanings, one with a positive connotation of "long-term," as in enduring the ages. The other means dealing with a negative situation, as in enduring the pain. Both definitions are necessary for commitment to a marriage—and that is required of *both* people. The Bible says not to be "unequally yoked." How well put is that? Think of two oxen sharing a yoke, pulling a wagon. That's a lot like life, eh? If one constantly does all the pulling, the wagon just goes in a circle—nowhere.

As a Type A person, I've always been self-directed. I don't need to ask others what they think about something to know what I think. I have a strong sense of what is right and wrong. I've tried but not always succeeded to just do the right thing and not worry about the rest. That probably sounds egotistical, arrogant, or selfish. It also follows that I don't think much about how other people feel about a given situation. I can appreciate how people perceive a situation, but how they feel is a bit analytical for me.

I do try to be sensitive, and doing the right thing means appreciating the impact of your actions and words on others, but I'm not really what you call a giving or sensitive guy. One associate surprised me when he described me to another person as intense. I just thought that I cared about the quality of the work product!

I say all of this to set the tone for how Darlene's battle with cancer impacted me and our relationship. It is my desire in this effort to give other cancer caregivers a point of reference from which to build a support structure that is helpful to the patient while at the same time allowing the caregiver a frame of reference to deal with his or her own issues evolving from the battle. Whether the caregiver is a spouse, family member, or friend, although he or she is not in the battle zone, that person provides the support without which the combatant cannot fight as he or she must.

As Darlene said, we had just become empty nesters after all the years of raising children and being very involved in their schedules. All parents know that raising children is not a part-time hobby. It is a full-time commitment and requires putting them first while what the parent wants to do is put on hold for about eighteen years as the parent tries to raise them and teach them how to build their own identity and character and make their way independently in this world. Then a parent has to loosen the apron strings and allow them to make decisions based on the values and life template he or she has taught them.

Like most folks, Darlene and I were caught up in the business of college expenses, functions, our professions, church activities, etc. We had experienced all the typical stress of most families, but we were committed to each other and to the marriage. When the girls went to college, we also expected to do some of the things we had put on hold. Some of those things for me were hunting, fishing, gardening, and just having some free time during which every minute of the day wasn't obligated.

As an attorney, I've lived my entire professional life documenting every day in the tenth-of-an-hour increments the clients require for billing. (Try it sometime, and see how your day is actually productive.) I have ambition coupled with a keen desire to always do my best. I am intense. My hobbies and fun stuff had been really pared back while our girls were in high school with all their activities, so I looked forward to some personal time while the girls were in college. Darlene had her own set of desires that had been put on hold, and we both looked forward to sharing some quality time together, doing fun stuff.

I had just finished a deposition in Aberdeen when I got the call from Darlene. I drove straight to the Memphis clinic, where everyone was very somber. I'd always thought breast cancer was quite treatable if caught early, and Darlene had always had annual physicals. She'd just been declared healthy a few days before finding her lump, so how bad could it really be, even if it was cancer?

You know what happened next. With that diagnosis, we just dropped everything, prayed, and focused a war on the disease that had attacked our family with intent to kill.

Every person is different and has to approach the hard things of life as he or she sees best. I am, however, surprised to see some react with simple resignation: *That is my fate; I accept it.* Some are so intimidated or overwhelmed that they just don't know how to respond, so they take the easiest or most readily available course of response. I hope this book will encourage anyone faced with a hard challenge to seek out the best information, doctors, consultants, and treatments he or she can get. You never know the outcome until the end—something these doctors at MD Anderson taught us.

When we left for Houston that Thursday, we had about three days' clothes apiece. We never thought it would be a full year before Darlene moved home again. My cases had to be put on hold for a while. People would just have to understand, and if not, they'd have to get over it or find somebody else because my first commitment was to my wife and family. As for my work, it went on. As managing member of our small firm, I also felt those around me at work needed to see how I was going to deal with this new issue. My witness to them would come from how I handled what they fully expected to be the slow death of my wife.

The lawyers and judges were understanding to a point, but the world doesn't stop just because you are dealing with cancer. The rest of the world keeps on turning, so you have to as well. Indeed, we were blessed to have many friends and family who came and stayed with Darlene in Houston, allowing me to carry on with work and manage our home. During her battle, our schedule settled into me working during the week and then flying out three weekends a month. It's a hard time, but you just have to remember to count your blessings and realize that for centuries, most people worked sixteen to eighteen hours a day just to survive in the most meager circumstances. The worst of today is better than the best of three hundred years ago or of the Depression era.

My main job, especially where Grace and Meredith were concerned, was to demonstrate how to respond to serious adversity. I felt an overwhelming obligation to show them leadership and character, which helped me shape my actions and reactions to events because I could not stand the thought of not being the daddy they had in their minds. So while Darlene fought for her life, my job was fighting to support her and show the girls how to deal with it.

No matter what happened with Darlene, my daughters would always have the knowledge of how I had responded to the challenge. How would my actions impact their ability to respond when faced with similar challenges that life would inevitably bring them? My job as their dad was to teach them how to live in this world. What an opportunity and responsibility! I knew how they would remember their mom and her courage. What memories would they have of their dad?

There was no place to commiserate on what this did to my plans for life. When one member of a family has cancer, the whole family has cancer. I believe this is the type family God has ordained; a physical family provides support for those who need it in the same way a spiritual family shares the load! Is your relationship with your spiritual Father such that you can discuss your problems with the One who already knows them?

My days and weeks ran together. I worked and then went home and tried to decompress to deal with the next day. I don't talk with others much about my personal life, and for twenty years, I had been in a house with three women, so there wasn't much opportunity to get a word in even had I wanted to. And they didn't much know how to discuss how fun it was to stand in ice water all day chasing something with feathers any more than I could tour forty-seven stores in a mall without breaking out in hives!

I did find a great conversationalist at home in an old, often overlooked friend, Beaureguard. Bogie was our other family member and the only other male in the house. Even though he was about seventy-seven years old, we could communicate well, since those were dog years and he mainly listened to my discussions while he sat in my lap or at my feet to show me the affection that counterbalanced my frustration of the day. Bogie was our miniature Schnauzer who had been the girls' pet as they grew up. Now he was my buddy as I grew old. He had his own problems—arthritis, missing teeth, eyes going bad—and he had to depend on me for his food and water, but he was faithful as always and very understanding, even when I was blatantly wrong. Sometimes Bogie would listen to Darlene on the phone, but mostly, he comforted me at night when I was alone.

I prayed a lot for understanding. I wanted to submit to God's ultimate will, even if that meant losing the fight. It's hard to say, "Thy will be done" when you recognize that will may mean the loss of your loved one. However, until you surrender the outcome *completely* to God, you will never be able to have any peace. When you can't pray, go to the Psalms and the prayers of the saints, which are there for a reason. After a while, the depth of both the physical and mental fatigue got to the point where I could not pray actively, so I adopted Psalm 23 from my days as a youth. Pray it slowly, and think of each line in depth. God listens.

Surrender is something that does not come easily to goal-oriented people. I was taught that you can accomplish whatever you determine if you work at it hard and long enough. Surrender was not my game plan, especially since I was determined to do anything and everything I could to defeat the cancer that attacked the woman I loved. The problem was that no matter how hard I tried or how badly I pursued the outcome, there really was nothing my personal efforts could do to change the outcome one whit. The option of surrendering it to God was made all the more difficult because I wasn't surrendering a goal or personal objective; I was surrendering the outcome of the battle for the life of my wife.

I repeated Psalm 23 to myself a lot. I changed my screen saver on my computer to "This Is Temporary," which is appropriate, I think. *Everything* in life is temporary; that fact is really important for us to understand and assimilate. The things we worry about every day—money, time, jobs, stress, sickness, friendships, schedules, business—are temporary, even death. It remains my screen saver today to remind me that all of *this* life is temporary, and like the morning vapor, our physical lives will soon be gone.

The diagnosis of cancer puts you in a frame of mind that naturally makes the whole family sensitive to everything. For the patient and the primary caregiver, that means coping with irrational side effects, emotional roller coasters that are aggravated by powerful drugs used for treatment, and then drug for treatment of the side effects of the treatment! Chemo is actually a very potent poison. Administration is managed but still makes the patient sick with side effects that are really just physiological responses to poison.

Those who try to help end up catching the brunt of the fatigue and pain, and sometimes it's hard for the caregiver to respond with kindness when the best effort put forth is not good enough. It's as if the patient has just rejected your most precious gift, but you have to remember that the patient isn't fully responsible due to the poison in his or her system. The patient is an unwilling prisoner in a cage with huge bars and jagged fencing that he or she cannot escape, so that person must endure the treatment. It is understandable that patients will sometimes lash out at their caregivers like a tiger that wants its freedom but can't get it.

At some points in time, it's your job as the caregiver to be the pin cushion and just receive the anger, frustration, hurt, and sometimes downright meanness that comes out. The frustration has to go somewhere, and at the time, nobody is saintly enough to be objective enough to know it's not really about what he or she has said or done, especially for a Type A who thinks he should be able to achieve a good result if he just works at it hard enough. The caregiver's reward is to assuage the patient, and sometimes that reward is difficult to get no matter how hard you try. You just have to love them through it.

Once, when Darlene was very sick from chemo, we got into an argument, and I responded with, "I did not give you cancer!" She, of course, knew that, but she was exhausted and sick and needed understanding, compassion, and my selflessness. She also needed to put forth extreme effort to overcome her symptoms and not allow herself to take it out on those around her. We all treat our families, the people who love us most and do the most for us, worse than we do mere friends. It is too much to expect that a person in the fight of his or her life, exhausted, sick, and in pain, can avoid lashing out from time to time. Sometimes it's just over how you fixed the eggs that morning, the television program you watch, or nothing. But even though the caregiver may sometimes feel that he or she is being treated unfairly, it's imperative to remember that nothing about cancer is fair. Fairness is for sissies, and this disease is the opposite of fair!

A few months after Darlene's surgery, we essentially forced a local doctor friend to drain a swollen place adjacent to one of the scars under Darlene's arm. It was a fairly large seroma, a pocket of fluid that accumulated under the skin from the surgery. *That* little experience took another three months to heal, with packing the wound twice a day with silver oxide gauze poked several inches into the wound so it would heal from the inside out. Again, it was tedious and unpleasant but just one of those things that was not cancer. So it was okay. You learn that although you may have to endure discomforts and problem issues, as long as it isn't cancer, you can deal with it. Throughout these complications, Darlene was always able to put her best face on the situation and work through the ordeals without asking for sympathy from others or using the situation as an excuse for anything.

The hardest parts of the battle for me were being completely powerless to do anything but pray and being supportive when the emotions and physical toll came due. Dealing with cancer and facing death are difficult for not only the patient, but also the entire family. You love the patient and care intensely about him or her, but that person's needs, wants, desires, demands, and expectations can get onerous and difficult to cope with. There is emotional and physical pain that is hard to put into words, but the spouse or caretaker has to carry on with the duties of living and working while attending to a very, very sick person. All the focus is on the patient, as it should be, but the spouse picks up a lot of the heavy lifting. Selfishness raises its head over and over, naturally, but there is no time or place for that.

Darlene was absolutely amazing in the way she addressed the fear of the diagnosis, treatment, and death sentence she was handed. She immersed herself in Scripture and positive thoughts, read uplifting books, and watched only lighthearted television shows. Character and courage are defined in the fire of battle, and it is imperative that the patient preserves all his or her energy to endure the treatment and fight the disease. I wish I could claim to have been a better support for this part of the battle, but the only thing of any substance I could do was pray that the Lord would provide her the strength of will and protect her from the demons of discouragement and outright despair.

As the caregiver, it is very important that you become the person you need to be to the patient as well as your family, the workplace, and yourself. You need a very clear understanding of who you are inside. It's a true test of character. Seeing the pain of both the physical treatment and the emotional pain of your loved one is hard. Gripping the idea that your wife won't see her children marry or see grandchildren and that your children won't have their mother in those very special times brings profound sadness that you simply *cannot* allow to take root while you fight the disease. The attitude has got to be, without waiver or exception, that we are here to fight the best fight we can until it is finished, one way of the other. There is no alternative; there is no choice.

The fight cannot be changed or questioned. As a caregiver, you must expect to be the one primarily keeping the can-do tone and support your patient emotionally as well as physically. God will reward your fight and help you, hopefully to absolute victory, but if not, then His will is sovereign and final, not to be questioned. What you do not want is to have any reason to look back and say, "If I had only ..."

All this focus on the fight needs to be tempered with the positive thought that you *can* win! It is easy to get so caught up in the daily grind of this most serious conflict that has enveloped you and your world that you forget there is a world that is unaffected by your situation. Try to maintain some semblance of contacts and activities that are fun. It's hard to find things to laugh at while you are so sick, but we all know laughter and uplifting thoughts are truly important.

Curiously, after the initial shock of the diagnosis and seeking a course of treatment, I somehow always felt a peace that Darlene was not going to die from her breast cancer—at least not then, not in the time normally allocated for her type of cancer. I sensed that it was going to be all right. I even told her that she would attend *my* funeral. Considering the fact that she was initially given a 2 percent chance of living more than one year, that was bold.

If I spoke to someone whose spouse or loved one had just been diagnosed with cancer, I would encourage that person to totally avoid the self-pity and questioning of God that rob you of energy to focus on the battle. This situation is not about the caregiver; it is about supporting a loved one as he or she personally wrestles with a demon named death.

Consider that this is a battle that may not be won but must be fought without compromise in order to have a *chance* to win. The burden of maintaining focus on the fight is with the caregiver. The patient is dealing with far too much to be expected to lead anybody else; that person is challenged just to stay alive and not to give in to the doubt, fear, and fatigue of the battle. None of us is entitled to expect to have, do, or avoid anything. Never ask why or how,. It doesn't make any difference anyway; the only thing that matters now is how you handle what you've been handed.

One of our friends—someone who, like me, is not known for being sensitive or empathetic—wrote Darlene some wonderful e-mails. He is not a particularly religious man, but God placed in his heart to write Darlene and tell her to endure. There's that word again. See it through to the end, outlast the enemy, don't give in, don't give up, and beat the enemy by being tougher for longer than it is. Often, this is as simple as making it through the current day. The only way you and your family can endure to the end is to look to God and Jesus Christ for your strength. Jesus Christ voluntarily endured the most heinous form of death simply because He loved us so much that it was worth it for Him in order for us to live. Faith in humans or anything short of the divine Jesus Christ, Son of God, will lead to disappointment.

He said, "You have not because you ask not" (James 4). He told us that as believers, we are, like Him, children of God. It is one thing to know He can perform miracles; it's another to have the faith that He will do it for you. I confess to being short on that level of faith. We are told to pray believing He will answer our prayers. The effectual, fervent prayer of a righteous man accomplishes much. Well, I'm not righteous beyond being a believer in Christ, and I'm not very good at being a Christian, but I do know that Jesus knows me and my family. If I counsel anyone who is battling cancer, my best advice is to make sure Jesus knows you and your family before you are called on to meet Him face-to-face.

Miracles do happen. I do not believe miracles are mere random anomalies or statistics, although those anomalies are out there. When we met with the doctors at MD Anderson, I told them they have the best medicine in all the world. They do. But God decides how well it will work in any patient's case. He decides—not us. We have no right to question His purposes—so don't. It's our duty to accept them, submit to Him, and set an example that lets others know that we know Him.

Absent His return before our physical death, we will all face death. Some of us will have a heads up; others will not. Those who die suddenly have been spared the lingering thought of the transition. It's harder for the family but easier on the dying. For those with forewarning, it's harder, but the family has a chance to say, "I love you." Let your loved one know that no matter the outcome, you are there for him or her, and then put your shoulder to the wheel and do your best to let that person know the outcome. Whatever it is, it will be okay.

This experience with Darlene has made me less focused on work and more focused on living—that's for sure. I also consciously try to consider her wants and desires more but probably am still just a dumb husband.

I realize now more than ever how special a person Darlene is to have endured what she has with such dignity and grace. Darlene has always been special to me and her family, but God has allowed me to see that she is truly an example and inspiration to many.

We were too busy to have a bucket list before Darlene's diagnosis, as we were working and focusing on the children. After the diagnosis, the bucket list got really simple: smell the rain and the flowers, feel the cool breeze, slow down, and watch the sun set and rise again. We promised to enjoy being still and truly appreciate the daily blessings of life and God's creation all around us.

When you have finished fighting cancer, you don't get greedy.

"The Lord is my Shepherd. I shall not want" (Psalm 23:1).

Chapter 25

What I've Learned about Relationships

Your personal relationship with God and your relationships with others are the most important treasures you have in your life. This is especially true when going through a difficult time.

After cancer, my idea of how to love and support others through difficult times changed a little bit. When I was on the receiving end of extravagant giving, I began to accept that allowing others to help me blessed them as well.

We were wired up for relationships, and sometimes God sends people into our lives when we are so devastated that it is hard to function or even pray. It's okay to not be able to pray, to hurt so badly, mentally or physically, that all you can do is cry. I really believe that an agonized "Oh, God" is a prayer. That's when you lean on others to pray for you.

If you haven't faced a crisis or time of difficulty yet, at some point, you will. (Take a deep breath.) Hopefully, you have a supportive family; if not, then perhaps you have a wonderful group of friends or church family on whom you can depend.

Family, friends, church family—one or all—serve as a source of comfort and invaluable support in times of pain, heartache, and struggle.

The bottom line is that a strong support group doesn't just happen. Relationships of all kinds thrive on attention, time, and love. People *need* each other. You need them now, and you will really need them later.

In the months prior to my diagnosis, I realized I'd not done enough to express my love and appreciation to my friends or to nurture relationships. I wanted to do a better job, so I made a commitment to mail one card every Monday morning to my friends, some of whom were sick or going through hard times. I'm just like everyone else—pressed for time—but it only took a few minutes to jot a quick note: "Thinking of you ..." "I appreciate you ..." "Miss you ..."

I love cards more now than even before cancer. I'll tell you why. The idea of the thank-you note was drilled into my head as a Southern child. It was one of the worst offenses to not acknowledge any gift, however small, without writing a proper thank-you note! Southern habits die hard, and I received many gifts from friends while I underwent treatment. I was delighted by and appreciated each and every gift, but I felt like I *had* to write a thank-you note for each one. *Ha!* Even while dealing with cancer, there's no reprieve from the thank-you note. I came to have a whole new appreciation for cards. I relished the thought behind a card and handwritten note, the fact that someone had taken the trouble to pick it out for me, address, and mail it. And most of all , no thank-you note was required!

From a time before I can remember, Mop and Pop instilled in me the need to go out of my way for others. Yes, working in the drugstore seeded the principle of hard work in my heart; but taking meals or a bag of clothes to a family struggling after a death or hurting during the holidays taught me the value of reaching out to others. This was something I've always prioritized with my children. I wanted them to grow up like I did, with the need to share our blessings with others. Never in my wildest dreams did I think we would be on the receiving end.

We change over time. So do friendships. Some grow closer; some grow farther away. I sometimes wonder if the friend is the one growing farther—after all, we all grow. What I do know is that time is limited. Cherish what you have, and don't dare hesitate to send cards, e-mails, or make phone calls to make peace with those you've had conflict. Each breath we take is a gift that we're not promised.

Forgive—really let go. This is hard for women to do, especially when something has to do with their children or husband! Jesus tells us to forgive over and over again in love. My approach had been to distance myself from anyone who did or said something hurtful. Friendships have too many blessings to forfeit if you ignore the elephant in the room. And guess what? You may be the only person who can see the elephant. They take up too much space. Just let it go.

What I've Learned about Waiting

Waiting requires that I relinquish control. It takes me out of the driver's seat. Waiting interrupted my plans and schedules and made me realize I couldn't drive anything, especially my life. I've always had a full agenda, and waiting was never a part of it. Without being given a choice, this unwanted event reminded me of who I am and who God is. Everything about my life—about life in general—became simpler. It had to.

During this process of becoming simpler, my radar became much more focused. Prayer, the gift of music, time with God, and time with friends and family became more precious than ever; those things had always been important in my life, but never so much as during my battle with cancer.

So many activities on our to-do lists can get in the way of what's important and what isn't. Anything in our lives that we do—even be good deeds—that takes away from time alone with God and listening to Him is not what He wants. As I've said before, my life pre-cancer was filled with to-do lists, a hectic pace, and sometimes even chaos. God is never the author of chaos— even organized chaos. "Those who cling to useless idols forfeit the grace that could be theirs" (Jonah 2:8).

When our daughters were still at home with us, they did everything. They were involved in many activities at school, church, and in the community—too many. In those days, I carried a color-coded calendar to help me know who had to be where at every hour of the day! Jay and I wanted (as I think most parents do) for the girls to experience athletics, the arts, church activities, mission work—everything possible—so as to discover their passion and purpose in life. They had a wonderful childhood, but that's the one aspect I'd change. The pace would have been slower. There would have been more down time, more time to just be.

Yes, my waiting was forced upon me, but in the process, I learned the incredible value of being still, praying, and listening. I had always been a praying woman but not a "sitting still and listening woman." I have also never encountered the comfort of God's Scriptures or the peace that everything was going to be okay until I was still long enough to recognize it. God tells us we will always have enough, that He gives us everything we need to deal with any circumstance we encounter. The amazing thing is that going into this, on that long night drive to Houston, I did not have enough. I never felt like I did; now, on the other side, I can see that the times of the most personal growth were the times I could only take life moment by moment, putting one foot gently in front of the other, leaning on God for the strength.

From the very beginning, I made up my mind that even though I didn't have a choice about waiting, I did have a choice in how I waited. I could be fearful, anxious, and have a pity party, or I could wait in hope, believing and trusting God. One day, almost near the end of radiation treatment, I was in an outpatient clinic, riding an escalator down to the next floor. A woman behind me was trying to speed up and walk while the escalator was moving. I turned to her and smiled but thought, *Isn't it hard to just be still and let the escalator carry you?* I immediately thought of how much I'd changed and learned.

All we have to do is be still and let God steer us through the rough water. Yet that is very hard to do! I didn't even know I needed downtime, and I sure didn't want it. Cancer hit me from my blind side and rocked my world to pieces. It was as if I was forced to patiently put together a gazillion-piece puzzle without a picture to look at. It turns out that the pieces were a better fit when I stopped trying to hurry and force them. And the finished picture looks completely different than I'd imagined.

What I Learned about Getting to Okay

"But he said to me, 'My grace is sufficient for you, for my power is made perfect in weakness.' Therefore I will boast all the more gladly about my weaknesses, so that Christ's power may rest on me" (2 Corinthians 12:9). Almost any cancer survivor (especially one who has faced a poor and frightening prognosis) will tell you that the key to sanity and survival is coming to a place of peace. It's okay, no matter the outcome.

Getting to that place is also critical in fighting the paralyzing fear that comes when staring at what is quite possibly the end of your life. Fear prevents one from seeing with clarity the beginning to the end, only allowing us to focus on the moment.

I had to get to a place of peace to realize that our time on this earth is just a blip, that God is and has always been sovereign, and that we will be with Him in the end. This is temporary. Be okay with whatever happens—maybe not because you're able to see things clearly, but because you know who has numbered our days. This is easier said than done, right?

I prayed and asked God for wisdom, clarity, understanding, and the faith to believe Him more. It has nothing to do with philosophy, intelligence, or rationalization. None of us is able to wrap his or her mind around the concept of time where God is concerned. It is simply outside of the abilities of our earthly minds to comprehend. Time, as we know it, has nothing to do with eternity. It only functions to remind us of the temporary.

I wanted to understand the big picture, to have a peace about my battle with cancer. I wanted to leave my family with the legacy that I didn't just roll over in self-pity, ask, "Why me?" and give up. I wanted them to know I'd done everything possible, but in the end, whatever the outcome, it would be okay.

Pre-cancer, I had been involved in countless Bible studies, and as a believer, I thought I already had a pretty good understanding of the big picture, God, eternity, and how our lives on earth are but vapor, a mist that quickly vanishes (James 4:14). But I didn't.

Until we're faced with death, most of us would rather not think about our own immortality. If you haven't heard, I hate to break it to you: we all die. It isn't a morbid acceptance, knowing I have no control; rather, it's a relief. God tells us He has ordained every day for us to wake up and take a breath before we are even born (Psalm 139:16). Yes, our days are numbered, but of course, this does not mean giving up a fight!

One of the worst scenarios I've witnessed is when someone I knew, diagnosed with cancer, said, "I'm not going to do anything or fight. This must be the end for me." How horrible is that? Her three children are suffering.

I didn't want to leave that kind of legacy for Meredith and Grace. When you make a decision to fight at the point of diagnosis, it's truly an unselfish choice because you're thinking of the impact on the family. I desperately wanted my girls, Jay, my parents, and my family to know that I was going to do whatever I had to do. Whatever happened was okay, and I was not going to cry constantly and crumble. I didn't want them to remember me that way. The choices one makes regarding health care and treatment affect not only the patient, but also family and friends. For me to fight most effectively, it was necessary to take an unconventional path and move to another city far from home.

Cancer isn't the only thing that can suddenly turn your world upside down. Maybe it's a sudden death, car accident, divorce, or even depression that brings about paralyzing fear. When you are stuck in that fear and can't even look legitimately at viable options, some people, instead of becoming advocates for themselves, make the wrong decisions, like choosing treatment at home simply because it's home and therefore familiar and easier or choosing to do nothing, so frozen in fear that decisions of any kind seem impossible. At times like those, you must somehow pull yourself up by your bootstraps. You just might find that you had more strength than you thought.

Getting to a place of peace and understanding is not about putting a plastic smile on your face and pretending that your situation is not hard. It is also *not* about courage or temperament. People make me incredibly uncomfortable when they say, "You have so much courage," "I wish I could be more like you," or "That's just how you are." That's wrong! God doesn't give wisdom only to the brave, the Type A's, the optimists, or the realists; He offers it to everyone and anyone who asks! "If any of you lacks wisdom, you should ask God, who gives generously to all without finding fault, and it will be given to you" (James 1:5).

I once had a conversation with a friend who was diagnosed with a terrible form of cancer. He told me, "Darlene, I can't be like you. I can't ask people to pray for me. I know I'm going to die. I just want to be left alone." He attributed my surviving to personality. I couldn't find the words to change his mindset. I'm still haunted by that conversation.

In the depths of the valleys, we must remember that God is the author of healing and miracles. And there's nothing wrong with praying for them or believing that He'll perform things that seem impossible to us but are as simple as breathing to Him. You may ask as I do, "If God intends for everyone to be healed, why are there people who must live this life paralyzed? Why do people go through agonizing suffering? Why do people even wear eye glasses or hearing aids? Am I not healed because my faith simply is not strong enough?" The apostle Paul (who certainly didn't lack faith) prayed three times for a thorn in his flesh to be removed. God did not answer his prayer with a yes but explained, "My power is made perfect in weakness" (2 Corinthians 12:9).

For any battle or fear you face, that is the key to getting through, whether you survive physically or not, whether the outcome is good or not. God's grace is sufficient.

At some point during the summer of 2004, it became clear to me that God had been preparing me for my battle, and it was a pivotal moment. He was in control, and nothing was going to touch me that didn't first go through His hands. I knew that it might be the end of my life, but I would be with Him. I had to know and see that or I couldn't have moved forward in my treatment, in requesting prayers from so many people and churches, and in talking openly and vulnerably to other people. For me, battling cancer was a journey I had to accept, and I wanted to be a witness for Him even when I didn't feel like it. I gave myself no choice but to rise to the occasion, confident that He would provide the strength. And once again, He proved faithful.

However, if a patient believes this is his or her time, the end of his or her life on earth, let that person go. Use this time for goodbyes rather than insisting on new doctors and treatments. After all, only God knows the plan. Only God knows the number of our days.

"For I consider that the sufferings of this present time are not worthy to be compared with the Glory that is to be revealed to us" (Romans 8:18). "I have fought the good fight, I have finished the course, I have kept the faith; in the future there is laid up for me the crown of righteousness, which the Lord, the righteous Judge, will award to me on that day; and not only to me, but also to all who have loved His appearing" (2 Timothy 4:7–8).

What I Learned about Standing in the Gap

Cancer affects many more than the patient. My diagnosis was like an implosion, radiating out and also hitting, hurting, testing, challenging, changing, and strengthening my husband, daughters, parents, siblings, and friends. That implosion is felt in any life-altering scenario, when your world is suddenly ripped apart or turned upside down, when the ones you love most are carried along automatically and unwittingly for the ride due only to their love for you.

Relationships are tested. Those I love have seen me at my worst, but they've also been with me in moments of unbelievable triumph. They've also laughed really hard in the middle of some of the toughest moments because life stuff still happens, and it is just funny. Lessons are learned, invaluable wisdom is gained, and bonds are strengthened.

Several of my friends have come together to help compile the material for this chapter. In writing this book, I started out strictly writing a resource for those going through the hard stuff and their caregivers and friends. I wish there was a way to depict the unfailing love and support they gave me. The best way I can figure is to provide some advice to others so that another person in the battle can have what I had in my life-altering situation.

Of course, what you say is determined in a large part on your relationship with the person who has been diagnosed. But in any case, even if it's your best friend and your sister, do not ask too many questions. At the beginning, this person has been traumatized. If you speak to this person during the first couple of days after diagnosis, he or she is probably still just trying to figure everything out for himself or herself. The most important thing is to keep the focus on the patient and not on your need to know all the details. Some people are very forthcoming and will give you details regarding stage, size, class, etc. when they tell you about the diagnosis.

No one really knows what to say, but here are some things you do not say:

- "I know how you feel"—unless you have had the exact same experience. It doesn't count if your sister, aunt, or favorite cousin has been through it. If you have not had it yourself, just don't go there.

- "Well, my friend's sister had it and she …" Later, the patient might want to hear some positive, encouraging things about cancer survivors, but if he or she has just been diagnosed, it's all about that person, and another's experience is just not going to be helpful.
- "Oh my God!" That's just not a good thing to say for obvious reasons.
- "Are you going to have reconstruction?" It's none of your business.
- "The Lord never puts more on us than we can bear; He will see you through this." That translates to "This is God's fault. He gave you the cancer, and He will heal you." We all know good Christians who have not won their battles.
- "Everything is going to be okay; I just know it." Things are *not* okay and may not ever be okay.

Don't be afraid to say something. Sometimes people were very afraid to mention cancer, even though everyone knew what they we thinking. Simply saying you are thinking of the patient or praying for him or her is much better than pretending the situation is not happening.

Really, just listen. The person who has been diagnosed needs to know by your behavior that you do not consider it a death sentence (even if you are convinced it is, like I was). But you don't want to treat the person like he or she just told you what he or she had for lunch either. Mainly you just want to say, "I'm so sorry you have to go through this," and then shut up and listen.

Do talk about it. At least acknowledge it, and open the opportunity for dialogue. I have some wonderful friends who always mentioned it, even if just through that extra hug and quietly saying, "Still praying." They understood the harsh reality of the odds against us but encouraged hope and faith that those odds could be beat.

There were also friends who maybe didn't feel comfortable being quite so intimately and emotionally involved but offered support and acknowledgement through sending cards or books, sometimes funny and sometimes serious. One friend, who has always been quite the fashionista, went out and found the best-looking hats I've ever seen and sent a whole boxful out to Houston for me. She was a friend who may not have always wanted to go through every detail of the treatments but whose eyes brimmed with sweet, love-filled tears when we talked. She demonstrated how much she loved us and cared in ways other than words.

No matter which avenue you choose to encourage those in need, pick one, and go for it. Don't be afraid and do what is never a good option: nothing. As said many times before, we are made for relationships. Kindness is never overrated. And who knows? Maybe it's you who'll soon need the shoulder to lean on.

What I've Learned about Humor

Laughter really can be the best medicine. And some things in life are just funny.

Chapter 26

Density

By now you may be wondering, *How in the world did a woman who had dutifully gone for annual mammograms since the age of forty for a period of ten years find herself in the worst possible cancer scenario?* In this chapter, I want you to learn what to look and listen for and expect and require from yourself as well as your healthcare provider. I don't want you to miss the signs.

Before I start explaining the *how* of my situation, I want everyone to understand that choosing a place of treatment is a very personal decision. Not everyone wants or is able to undergo treatment so far from his or her home. For me, there was no choice other than a hospital devoted solely to the treatment of cancer because my breast cancer was stage four, meaning there is no standard protocol. I have many friends who've been diagnosed with cancer who were treated close to their homes in local hospitals with wonderful results. But those friends were diagnosed at stage one to three, a diagnosis that is not nearly so final, where the cancer has not yet moved through the lymphatic system and landed on other organs. Their cancer was contained, and a standard protocol worked just fine for them.

I am insistent, however, when someone calls me for advice and they've received the news that their cancer is stage four, that the patient seeks a center of excellence, meaning a research institution devoted to cancer. It's an incredibly difficult decision for a patient to leave his or her home, family, and friends behind for the uncertainty of cancer treatment, but with a stage four diagnosis, there is really no other choice. I was incredibly blessed that my children were older; I don't know how I would have left my girls for a year of treatment if they had been toddlers. I like to think that I would have had the strength to make a short-term sacrifice of one year of treatment in order to gain many more years with them. I've met many young mothers who face that very predicament, and it's a gut-wrenching decision.

Many people also have the misconception that a center devoted solely to the treatment of cancer is financially unattainable for them. This is untrue. My insurance, Blue Cross Blue Shield, paid for treatment at MD Anderson just like it would have for anything else near my home. There are also an incredible number of resources, such as groups of churches that own furnished apartments for cancer patients and their families, near MD Anderson that rent for a fraction of the normal rent in Houston. Some of these same churches even deliver food, and there is transportation available to and from the medical center.

I had been told repeatedly over years that I had dense breast tissue. But I didn't know what that *meant* and certainly didn't know the significance. I consider myself to be an educated person; my career is in the healthcare field, and I actually worked in the hospital where I had most of my mammograms.

When the radiologist told me I had dense breast tissue, I thought to myself, *Why, thank you.* And then I'd proudly go home and tell Jay the news, because I thought I'd just received a great compliment! I thought it meant that I still had the breasts of a teenager. *Ha!* It never crossed my mind, especially with no history of breast cancer in my family, that I should have requested additional testing in the form of an MRI or ultrasound. Dense breast tissue, I later learned, simply meant that my mammograms were difficult to read.

Research has unanimously shown that women who have dense breast tissue are at increased risk for breast cancer[1,2]. *Komen.org* explains, "Breast density refers to the proportions of fat and tissue in the breasts as seen on a mammogram. High breast density means there is a greater amount of tissue compared to fat. Low breast density means there is a greater amount of fat compared to tissue. Women with very dense breasts, as seen on a mammogram, are four to six times more likely to get breast cancer than women with low breast density." To be clear, the American Cancer Society explains that mammographic density does not correlate with tissue hardness, as in a clinical exam.

Not only is breast density an independent risk for breast cancer, but mammographic density (MD) also impacts the detection of cancer by mammogram screenings, especially density greater than 50 percent.[3] According to an American College of Radiology Imaging Network (ACRIN) study published in a 2008 *Journal of the American Medical Association,* not only do more than half of women younger than fifty have dense breast tissue (as do one-

---

[1]   Boyd NF, Guo H, Martin LJ, et al. Mammographic density and the risk and detection of breast cancer. N Engl J Med. 356(3):227-36, 2007.

[2]   Tamimi RM, Byrne C, Colditz GA, Hankinson SE. Endogenous hormone levels, mammographic density, and subsequent risk of breast cancer in postmenopausal women. J Natl Cancer Inst. 99(15):1178-87, 2007.

[3]   Crystal P, et al. Using sonography to screen women with mammographically dense breasts. AJR 1003; 181:177-182

third of women older than fifty), but mammography's sensitivity for women with dense breast tissue also can be as low as 30 to 48 percent, with higher interval cancer rates and worse prognosis for the resulting clinically detected cancers.[4] The MD was also directly associated with more aggressive tumor characteristics subsequent studies. [5],[6]

Since I was diagnosed more than ten years ago, mammography has benefited from pivotal improvements, specifically digital mammography. Digital mammography is better at detecting cancer in women who are premenopausal, perimenopausal, women younger than fifty, or women who have dense breast tissue. The images aren't much different from plain film, but they can be viewed in different ways on a computer. They can be lightened or darkened, and certain spots of concern can be enlarged to examine more clearly. The images can also be stored or shared more easily for review by another radiologist.

I never had a digital mammogram. The technology was unavailable in my area at that time. Almost all facilities now have digital mammography available. Ask. You need to know what type of technology is being used. Studies have shown, however,

---

[4]   Berg, et al. Combined Screening With Ultrasound and Mammography vs Mammography Alone in Women at Elevated Risk of Breast Cancer. Journal of the American Medical Association. JAMA. 2008;299(18):2151-2163. doi: 10.1001/jama.299.18.2151 (http://jama.ama-assn.org/content/299/18/2151.abstract?sid=2c3c0da9-b1fd-45a4-ab56-d9995b2a6758)

[5]   Yaghjyan L, et al. Mammographic breast density and subsequent risk of breast cancer in postmenopausal women according to tumor characteristics. J Natl Cancer Inst. 2011;103(15):1179-89

[6]   Bertrand KA, et al. Mammographic density and risk of breast cancer by age and tumor characteristics. Breast Cancer Research. 2013 15(6):R104

that women with highly dense breast tissue unfortunately do not benefit as much as others from this newer technology.[7]

Breast density is not constant. It changes over time, dependent on numerous factors—such as childhood obesity, childhood height, genetics, and hormone therapy, among many others—all of which are currently under intense research. Rutter, et al reported that the increasing use of hormone therapy amplifies the problem of breast density since initiation and discontinuation of hormone replacement therapy affect density. That study reported that density increases with initiation and decreases with discontinuation of estrogen therapy.[8]

And always, always request a copy of your medical records for your own file, but especially request a copy of the radiologist's reading, a written report of your mammogram. This report is more detailed than a letter you might receive from your OBGYN or family doctor that tells you you're all clear and "we'll see you next year." In the radiologist's report, the doctor will indicate whether the patient has dense breast tissue. Request *(insist)* upon additional screenings if there is any indication that you have dense breast tissue, even if you have to pay out-of-pocket, for your peace of mind and to prevent any small beginnings of cancer being overlooked or missed outright. Like everyone else in the world, insurance companies are pinching pennies and choosing to limit funding for certain diagnostic tools. This is sad.

---

[7]   Berg, et al. Combined Screening with ultrasound and mammography compared to mammography alone in women at elevated risk of breast cancer: ACRIN 6666. JAMA 2008; 299(18): 2151-2163.

[8]   Rutter CM, et al. Changes in breast density associated with initiation, discontinuation, and continuing use of hormone replacement therapy. JAMA 2001;285:171-176

I Have Cancer. I Want To Live.

The American Cancer Society recommends annual mammography and MRI screening for women who are at very high risk for developing breast cancer.

Of course, I'm not the only woman whose breast cancer was undetectable because of dense breast tissue. Henda Salmeron, a native Texan, also self-discovered a nodule only six months after a normal mammogram. At the age of forty-three, Helda, a wife and mother of two children, was diagnosed with stage two breast cancer. I'm happy to report that Helda's health is wonderful, and she is the founding member of DENSE (Density Education National Survivors' Effort), a group of women advocating for breast density awareness nationwide.

The "Breast Density/Inform" law was passed in the state of Connecticut in 2009, mandating that patients be informed of their breast density. It has become the rallying point for the group, which consists of breast cancer survivors, all of whom received a later stage diagnosis than necessary because breast density interfered with the effectiveness of their mammograms. States like Florida, New York, Massachusetts, and Texas will have similar bills introduced in their upcoming state senate sessions, and legislators in California and Missouri will also research the issue. For more information, look for Henda's Law on Facebook or visit her website at *http://densebreasttissue.net/*.

While much research is ongoing regarding the benefits of increased screening techniques, controversy still surrounds the increased costs of these tests and reimbursements for medical professionals that do not justify the time and effort required to perform the tests properly. To be fair, some studies have shown there is no decrease in mortality by these additional screening tools. In addition, the new state laws mentioned above have caused debates over whether the government should dictate who should and should not have these tests.

182

A May 2010 national survey conducted by Harris Interactive for U-Systems, a company that develops breast ultrasound systems, found that 95 percent of women over the age of forty do not know their breast density, and nearly 90 percent did not know it increases the risk of developing breast cancer. Ask your doctor. Be informed.

I also started having trouble with premenopausal symptoms at the age of forty—hot flashes, inability to sleep, and crankiness. For three years, the symptoms only got worse, so I went to my gynecologist, who assured me it couldn't be menopause. I told him that my mother and grandmother had gone through menopause in their early forties as well. He encouraged walking regularly for exercise to help with the symptoms, as these were all common in women during menopause.

Later, frustrated when exercise and other remedies weren't helping, I went to another doctor in Memphis. He wrote me a prescription for a low-dosage birth control pill and said it would add in some hormones and help with symptoms, but he too was adamant that I could not be going through menopause.

Every year, when I went back to the same doctor for a checkup, I asked, "Shouldn't we check on this? How long do I keep taking these pills?" Finally, at age fifty, I asked the doctor, as he wrote me another prescription for twelve months of birth control pills, "Shouldn't we check my hormone levels, because as long as I'm taking this, we're really never going to know if I'm going through menopause or not? This is making me to continue to have a period."

He said, "Oh, we do need to do that and check your hormone levels." He made the appointment for lab work, but I never made it. It was too late.

I had no idea that the most common type of breast cancer is infiltrating ductile carcinoma, much of which is hormonally-driven, according to the National Breast Cancer Foundation. The estrogen I was putting into my body in the form of birth control pills only fed the cancer, and my doctors think the increased estrogen is why the cancer metastasized so quickly. Moreover, according to the *Journal for Clinical Oncology*, a woman with dense tissue's risk of breast cancer is increased with postmenopausal hormone therapy.[9]

I also bought over-the-counter medications with estrogen and soy to help with hot flashes and insomnia. Although suggested by manufacturers and marketed as a natural remedy, soy has not been shown in research to actually help with menopausal symptoms or increase the risk of breast cancer in numerous randomized controlled trials.[10] Always ask your doctor before taking anything over-the-counter to alleviate symptoms.

I don't blame anyone for my cancer being missed; rather, I blame a lack of education and awareness. Not one person warned me to the dangers of OTC medications that are not FDA approved, possible side effects, or implications of taking prescribed birth control pills for menopausal symptom relief or even suggested my hormone levels be checked regarding menopause. I realize hormone testing is not a standard practice for premenopausal women because estrogen levels fluctuate so much throughout the month, week, and even day, but hormone changes signal the onset

---

[9] Kerlikowske K, Cook AJ, Buist DSM, et al. Breast cancer risk by breast density, menopause, and postmenopausal hormone therapy use. *Journal of Clinical Oncology*. July 19, 2010.

[10] Nelson HD, Vesco KK, Haney E, et al. Nonhormonal therapies for menopausal hot flashes: systematic review and meta-analysis. JAMA. 295(17):2057-71, 2006.

of menopause. (What is more, estrogen is essential for healthy bones, heart, liver, and neural activity.)

According to *www.komen.org,*

> At this time, blood estrogen levels are not used by health care providers to assess breast cancer risk. However, there are certain markers that can be used to estimate how much estrogen you have been exposed to in your lifetime. For example, your age at your first period and your age at menopause indicate how many years you were exposed to higher estrogen levels related to menstrual cycles. All women can lower their estrogen levels by maintaining a healthy weight, limiting alcohol intake and being physically active.

For the seven years I took birth control pills, I was unaware of the mounting controversy and debate surrounding bioidentical hormones, which are hormones that are biochemically identical to those produced by the human body. In an ongoing federally-funded trial called the Women's Health Initiative, new evidence was released in October 2010 that linked synthetic hormone treatment as a combination of estrogen and progestin after menopause with an increased risk of breast cancer, more aggressive forms of breast cancer, and an increased death rate.[11]

Dr. Rowan Chlebowski, MD, PhD, professor at UCLA School of Medicine, and breast oncologist at the Los Angeles Biomedical Research Institute also examined postmenopausal women on combined therapy of estrogen and progesterone. In

---

[11] Writing Group for the Women's Health Initiative Investigators. Risks and benefits of estrogen plus progestin in healthy postmenopausal women: principal results from the Women's Health Initiative randomized controlled trial. JAMA. 288(3):321-33, 2002.

a podcast for a production of the *Journal of the National Center Institute,* Dr. Chlebowski said,

> We have just reported that estrogen plus progestin actually increases breast cancer mortality, as well, so taken together with our lung cancer results, estrogen plus progestin used for about five and a half years increased death from the two leading causes of cancer death in women, and because estrogen plus progestin interfered with breast cancer diagnosis, it kind of makes the breast denser, so the cancers were there, but were not able to be detected, so that meant they were able to grow and get to be a larger stage.[12]

My point: ask. Don't be afraid to ask your doctor any questions regarding any new medications or symptoms you have. And if you just don't feel right about something, seek other advice. Second opinions saved my life.

I don't say any of this to induce fear, uncertainty, or even distrust in your doctor. I never missed an annual appointment, pap smear, or mammogram, and I even did self breast exams most months. Remember, I found my area of concern while changing clothes. Though they have some risks, birth control pills also have some benefits, including preventing unwanted pregnancies and decreasing the risk of both uterine and ovarian cancers. Newer

---

[12] Journal of the National Cancer Institute Volume 102 Issue 18 Interview Transcript http://www.oxfordjournals.org/our_journals/jnci/podcast/transcript_interview_102-18.html

low-dose pills have limited research but so far show no link to increased risks of cancer.[13],[14]

And I certainly don't blame any of my doctors; they were thorough during exams. Now that I know the high-risk population for breast cancer, I know my history did not warrant further testing. For example:

- I had no history of breast cancer in my family.
- I had always been lean, and my onset of menarche was not until I was fourteen. Girls who had onset of menarche before the age of twelve have a 20 percent increased risk of breast cancer over those who had onset after the age of fourteen.[15]
- I had my first child before the age of thirty-five. Having the first child after the age of thirty-five increases risk.[16]
- I had more than one child; having more than one reduces risk.[17]

[13] Hannaford PC, Selvaraj S, Elliott AM, Angus V, Iversen L, Lee AJ. Cancer risk among users of oral contraceptives: cohort data from the Royal College of General Practitioner's oral contraception study. BMJ. 335(7621):651, 2007.

[14] Beral V, Doll R, Hermon C, et al. for the Collaborative Group on Epidemiological Studies of Ovarian Cancer. Ovarian cancer and oral contraceptives: collaborative reanalysis of data from 45 epidemiological studies including 23,257 women with ovarian cancer and 87,303 controls. Lancet. 371(9609):303-14, 2008.

[15] Kelsey JL and Bernstein L. Epidemiology and prevention of breast cancer. Annu Rev Public Health. 17:47-67, 1996.

[16] Rosner B, Colditz GA and Willett WC. Reproductive risk factors in a prospective study of breast cancer: the Nurses' Health Study. Am J Epidemiol. 139: 819-835, 1994.

[17] Anderson DE and Badzioch MD. Familial breast cancer risks. Effects of prostate and other cancers. Cancer. 72: 114-9, 1993.

- I began menopause before the age of forty-five, which also decreases risk.[18]

Be sure you know the warning signs, no matter what your risk is! The National Cancer Institute, American Cancer Society, and Centers for Disease Control and Prevention list the warning signs you should be aware of:

- lump, hard knot, or thickening in the breast or underarm area
- swelling, warmth, redness, or darkening
- change in the size or shape of breast
- dimpling or puckering in the skin
- itchy, scaly sore or rash in the nipple
- pulling in of the nipple or other parts of the breast
- nipple discharge that starts suddenly
- new pain or spot that doesn't go away

Cancer cells mutate all the time. The body almost always kills the mutant cells, but sometimes they get a foothold and form a tumor. Some mutant cells carry an estrogen receptor, and if your cancer is formed from cells with the estrogen receptor, they are fertilized by the estrogen. However, the amount of estrogen in the body does not correlate to initiating cancer because most breast cancer is found in postmenopausal women whose estrogen is naturally reduced, and pregnant women with extremely high levels of estrogen do not have increased breast cancer risks.

The amount of estrogen consumed by the estrogen receptive cancers is very small. (It doesn't take much estrogen.) So although

---

[18]   Missmer SA, Eliassen AH, Barbieri RL, Hankinson SE. Endogenous estrogen, androgen, and progesterone concentrations and breast cancer risk among postmenopausal women. J Natl Cancer Inst. 96(24):1856-65, 2004.

the cells eat estrogen, if you are taking estrogen supplements, you simply increase the amount of available estrogen; you don't increase the rate of cell division. Like a cow eating hay, it can only eat so much, no matter how many bales are available. However, if you have estrogen positive cancer, treatment includes trying to reduce the total amount of estrogen below the level of the cancer's appetite to weaken it.

People have asked me about genetic testing, if my girls have had it, and if I recommend it. The truth is, only 5 percent of women have the gene, and the gene testing isn't 100 percent accurate. But if you're among the 5 percent who have the gene, you're 80 percent more likely to develop breast cancer. I do not have the gene.

While my doctors do not know what causes a woman to develop breast cancer—or specifically, what caused mine—every case is different. Mammograms are used to screen people because they are relatively cheap, safe, and pick up some cancers early. However, it is not fair to lead people to think mammograms are more definitive than they really are. Medicine and cancer treatment are not objective sciences; there is a lot of art involved in determining how an individual should be treated. Society has become accustomed to the idea that medicine, like other things, should always have a perfect result or favorable outcome. This is unrealistic; life is not certain or predictable.

After at-length conversations with my primary oncologist and other doctors, they continued to emphasize that my treatment was exceptionally successful. But the next person with an identical diagnosis cannot expect the same result even if the exact same protocol was followed. Doctors often have to use a little art in explaining things, because many people will hear one thing, and for them, it becomes fact, when they actually misunderstood or failed to comprehend the totality and reality of what was said.

Saying somebody has dense tissue that makes the test more difficult to read is an honest statement and is communicated so that if the individual discovers a tumor, as I did, he or she will be less likely to think, *Well, the doctor missed it, and if he had found it earlier, I would have a better prognosis.* As my doctor said, most breast cancers have been in existence for many years before they are large enough to be discovered, and it's unreasonable to expect doctors to be perfect—but that's what society expects now. Just because a medical test or procedure had a bad result, it is not necessarily the doctor's fault. We simply will never have a perfect world where we can control all the outcomes—at least not in this lifetime.

This is why we need Christ. If we could make it on our own, we wouldn't need Him. Uncertainty and hard facts of life are forever realities in this life. One of the questions most people ask when bad things happen is, "Why me"? I just couldn't ask this; I had to ask myself, "Why not me?" "As he went along, he saw a man blind from birth. His disciples asked him, 'Rabbi, who sinned, this man or his parents, that he was born blind?' 'Neither this man nor his parents sinned,' said Jesus, 'but this happened so that the works of God might be displayed in him. As long as it is day, we must do the works of him who sent me'" (John 9:1–4).

It is comforting to know this. Under His sovereign plan, He allows us to endure trials and sickness only so that His glory may be revealed. The New Testament was originally written in Greek, not English. The Greek word actually used here for "displayed" is *phaneroo,* which means "to manifest." So we can translate this to mean "But let the works of God be manifested." This is a divine opportunity!

Moreover, I believe we must seek the best medical care possible. We must trust the brilliant doctors to help choose the best treatment for sickness. But we must also remember that hope is not found in statistics. Cancers with 97 percent survival rates have 3 percent death rates. No test is 100 percent sensitive, and no treatment is 100 percent effective. Nothing is sure except our source of hope, Jesus Christ, who gave His life so we could enjoy eternity with Him in heaven. Because of His grace, we are saved, not because of anything we've done (Ephesians 2:8–9). All we must do is believe in the Lord Jesus Christ, and we will be saved (Acts 16:31).

This book is intended to be a source of helpful information and hope. It is just my story. I pray it can give hope because the result was so wonderful, but too minute a discussion of the experience on a personal level might take the focus off the mission of conveying hope and help to trying or expecting to emulate and repeat the result. Thus, none of us knows our destiny and should not expect to repeat someone else's experience by copying his or her actions.

I hope people will recognize and utilize a few tools to handle the diagnosis and treatment while at the same time showing that the patient is not the only person. (It gets lonely facing and fighting cancer.) By doing everything you can, I hope you will see that you can still have a life and appreciate the life you have been given. And hopefully, more will have successful outcomes as a result.

Epilogue

Bogie, our girls' childhood pet and Jay's faithful companion, lived. He hung on until I made it back home for good. He was old and physically in tough shape, having escaped death several times. I'd been home about four months when he left us. One night, he went for his outside walk before bed and never came home. Dogs do that when they know their time is spent, and we understood. He was a great pet.

I went to visit the writer of the midnight prayer soon after I came home for good to try to express what her words of encouragement meant to me and my family. She said, "God is so good, and I've been calling your name to Him." In 2008, she went home to be with her Lord.

On July 5, 2005, Mop had her first birthday party—her seventieth! The Bouffants, a wildly popular cover band from Memphis, played and sang for hours—songs from the 1950s to the 1980s, complete with their trademark big hair and costumes. The party was a special surprise for Mop, and I think it was one of the highlights of her life.

Grace was attending college in Nashville after being admitted to the doctoral program of audiology at Vanderbilt when Mop, a huge supporter of the Miss Tennessee pageant, talked Grace into entering. Grace had only competed in a few pageants in junior high and high school, but she was crowned Miss Tennessee in 2007! She used her platform to bring awareness to not only the often-overlooked disability of hearing impairment, but also to tell my story of battling cancer.

It was another surreal moment when our family and a large group of Grenadians and friends went to Las Vegas as she competed in the Miss America pageant in 2008. She sang "What a Wonderful Day," which was written for breast cancer survivors. Grace was chosen for the top fifteen but was later eliminated. None of us cared. What a ride. What an experience—from cancer to Miss America.

In 2007, for Jay and my thirtieth wedding anniversary, we spent two weeks in Italy.

Flying makes me uneasy; I'd only traveled out of the country once, to Mexico. Jay thought I'd never get on the plane because of the distance, but after having cancer …

While on a boat going down Lake Como in Northern Italy, we passed little villages that looked like postcards and views of the snow-covered Swiss Alps, and it hit me—again. I closed my eyes and breathed deeply of the fresh air. Each breath is such a gift.

George Cloony has a house on Lake Como. I looked for him on a boat without his shirt on. *Ha!* The entire trip was slow and unhurried, like we were in a different world; it was surreal. The trip was only a year and a half after my battle with cancer. All through the trip, we kept looking at each other and saying, "Can you believe we're really here?"

In October 2009, I sat in the front row, again feeling extreme thankfulness and joy as Grace married Micajah Sturdivant at the Biltmore in Ashville, North Carolina. The views from the lawn were breathtaking, as was Grace in her dress as she walked through the blooming gardens on Jay's arm to the altar. This was another picture of God's grace. Not only did I have the privilege of dancing on the tables at Meredith's reception, but I also watched Grace marry the love of her life four years later!

In April of 2010, we celebrated another anniversary—my fifth anniversary of NED, a milestone for cancer patients. At the five-year mark, the reoccurrence rate drops significantly. After Cancerland, you celebrate two milestones each year, and I'll never dread another birthday again in my life. Most of my family was able to gather for an evening of food, thankfulness, toasting, reminiscing, and honoring the gift of life. Leo, my incredible brother, and his wonderful wife, Tonya, came and stayed with me several times throughout my stay in Houston. I call him my little brother, but the truth is that he's six foot five and has always been protective of me.

Leo's description of his toast at the five-year celebration:

> From the beginning, I thought a great deal about what Jay must be going through in that we are in similar situations; both of us lead partners in our respective law firms, both with two children still in college, both very reliant on our wives for so many things—busy

and rather stressed guys, to say the least. I think the impact of a diagnosis like Darlene's on the spouse is often overlooked. I thought Jay was the perfect example of what a husband should be during the entire ordeal.

His toast stated,

> We are here to celebrate Darlene's five-year anniversary, and I think it is the perfect occasion for me to make a toast to her husband, my brother-in-law, Jay. As the father of a daughter and the brother of two sisters, I can tell you that I am always highly skeptical of anyone who becomes their husband. As a lawyer for over twenty-five years, I realize from the beginning of any marriage that it's probably going to end badly. Statistically, that is the world in which we live. After Jay and Darlene had been married twenty years or so, I relaxed a bit, but you just never know. Then my sister was diagnosed with end stage cancer.
>
> Looking back, it is clear that Jay was the first to answer our family's prayers. He was with her every step of the way, helping make critical decisions, taking control of the situation when it was necessary, and always making Darlene's care and treatment the priority above all else. I know it must have been tempting to have taken the first doctor's advice and [have] her treated locally. It would have been so much easier. Going to a place like MD Anderson would cost so much more—and he's a real tightwad—and would make it so much more difficult on him. Nevertheless, he decided she should stay in Houston and receive the best treatment in the world—a choice that no doubt saved her life. Through the whole ordeal, he showed us

how it's done. So I just wanted to tell him tonight that he has finally made it. All my skepticism is gone, and I am so very thankful that he is a part of my family!

Once you've had cancer, life is never the same. Our family gets a reminder every four months when I go back to MDA for a battery of tests. These four months go by very quickly. Jay and I make a conscious effort not to live in fear, focusing instead on our many blessings. We still believe. We know that God ordains our days in this life. But every time we make the trek back to Houston, it's a tense time for our entire family. Every time, I'm anxious, scared, and almost ashamedly doubtful.

The ride out there is usually quiet and reflective, and we listen to the music all the way there. I don't think I could make the trip without the comfort of those songs. The ride home after the "all clear" is much different, as you can imagine. The relief is palpable. I've discovered that I must thank God for those feelings of helplessness, anxiety, and uncertainty so that I never forget the absolute miracle He performed in me and my family. Each day truly is a gift.

Our apartment angel, Kyle Wright, is now my Facebook friend. He's now a very successful attorney. And he's cut his hair.

God never fails to remind me of His promises. Since my year of treatment, I've shared my story at numerous churches, schools, and women's groups. At a Presbyterian church in Jackson, Mississippi in 2006, a young woman came up to me after I'd finished speaking. She had tears in her eyes as she told me about a particular part of my story—the rainbow. She was there that day, she told me, at MD Anderson with her mother. She saw the rainbow just after her mother passed away. But even in the beginning stages of grief, she told me she took comfort in the sight of God's love and promise. I could barely speak and thought of Jay's words, how everyone got meaning from the rainbow that day. Little did we know.

I'm now a member of the Anderson Network, and I probably answer two to three phone calls and e-mails each week from newly diagnosed patients, family members, and friends wanting to know what to do for their loved ones. Some are referred to me by the Network but others contact just because they've heard my story. Every phone call or e-mail takes me back. It is hard to relive and be constantly reminded of battling cancer, but nothing gives me greater joy than to share my experiences and help others realize that they are not alone in this journey.

Many of the women to whom I speak who've been diagnosed with cancer continue with their regular schedules of work, taking care of their children, and other obligations because they have no other choice. Some have young children and are forced to make that difficult choice of sacrificing time away from their children for life-saving treatment. Although it was hard to be away from my home, it was a luxury to be able to totally focus on my battle with cancer.

The women who have small children and still have to carry on some semblance of a normal life even in the midst of fighting cancer are my heroes. Young mothers have shared stories with me about their hopes for a normal day. Normal is what you hope for. They desperately want to be able to fold laundry, go to the grocery store, and pick their children up from school. I hope that if you know someone battling cancer, you now know what to do. The small things make a big difference.

⁓

On September 1, 2010, one of my greatest hopes and prayers was realized when I was able to greet Silas Jay and Avery Grace, my grandchildren. Meredith and Bruce are the proud parents of twins. They are the joy of my life. And as if God has not blessed our family enough, Grace and Micajah welcomed a daughter, Eleanor Gore, August 24, 2011 and Garnett Carruthers on August 15, 2013.

⁓

Last summer, I was driving on I-40 in Jackson, Tennessee on my way to visit to Mop and Pop. I had the music blaring my old favorites, "Made Me Glad" and "Be Still My Soul." I was transported back to April 2005, back to the radiation room and that table where I had to lie still. I was singing at the top of my lungs, happy tears were flowing down my face, and the choreography automatically took over my body. Truckers blew their horns at me!

My desire now in life is to tell people about my Lord who loved, saved, and healed me and that they can have this too. God has truly worked a miracle in my life! The truth is that my cancer could come back at any time, or I could get hit by a car tomorrow. Or I could live another twenty years. Death will happen to me just like it does to everyone. God is in charge of all my days. He knows the beginning to the end—what a comfort to know!

I've been granted more time on this earth with my family, and I'm filled with a joy that is hard to express. The closest I can come is with song and hand motions.

Afterword

With Meredith Gore Warf

It was a good place. We were in a good place, Bruce and I. The biggest joys of our lives had arrived eleven months before: Silas and Avery. We knew when we got married in 2005 that we wanted to wait a few years to have children and were ecstatic, not to mention shocked, to find out we were expecting twins due September of 2010. It was a wonderful nine months of pregnancy and incredulous day of happiness when Silas and Avery were welcomed to our world on September 1, 2010. They were the first grandchildren for my parents and came six years after mom had been told she would no longer be alive. Praise God.

Experiencing the blessing of children fills the heart with something that simply can't be described, much in the same way we think of falling in love. Watching Mom be victorious after her battle/war with cancer enjoy my own children is also something I can't describe.

Mom had been asked by countless people and our family to put her story on paper into a book for years. She had not felt a peace about starting that process until early 2010. We celebrated her five-year "birthday" in May of 2010 and began her book shortly thereafter. As you've read, she kept journals throughout her journey and selflessly agreed to share parts of them for the book. I took on the task of editing the project the summer after

Silas and Avery were born. (We were finally getting sleep at night, and life began to return to normal.)

Many weekend afternoons during the twins' naps, I would spend a few hours in the morning and a few hours in the afternoons with my computer and the manuscript, morphing my mind into what I thought was my mom and her character six years previously. This was mental, emotional, and physical exercise like I had never had before in all my years of sports, challenging academics, wifehood, or motherhood. This was also, much like the second year of my college days, a spiritual awakening for me. I truly wrestled with the Lord (again) about difficult concepts, unanswered questions, fears, and things that simply did not make sense. I did my best to enunciate my feelings on the computer screen staring at me, then leave it there and enjoy my precious children.

Everything was coming together, and I truly believe the Lord guided each step. Mom's story is one with sorrow, fear, faith, and triumph, of love and faithful demonstration of our Creator's divine sovereignty and unending love for us. We want to share that with others and pray it is an encouragement to them, pointing each co-laborer to our Lord and Savior, Jesus Christ, who offers us life eternally.

It was a good place. We had planned the twins' first birthday party as a small gathering with family the day before my sister, Grace, was scheduled to have her first child. A few days before, I had been outside on our deck, editing this book, when I looked down and noticed a red bump on my left upper thigh. Interestingly, I had never noticed it before. Small, red, smooth, symmetrical, it was nothing that we know of to be worrisome. I have gone to the dermatologist once a year since I was in college, mostly due to my light hair, fair skin, and light-colored eyes as well as a family history of basil cell carcinoma. My dermatologist always seems to take off one of my many moles and freckles, but everything is always okay. I was scheduled for my regular dermatologist exam three weeks later anyway, and I said to myself, "I'll get her to look at it if it's still there." After all, the spot really looked like a blister or irritation.

The twins' birthday party was a success, and my niece, Eleanor, was born beautifully healthy, and we all celebrated. The spot on my thigh did not change.

At the appointment three weeks after the spot appeared on my thigh, my dermatologist said, "I do not know what that is, but if it bothers you, I will take it off." Of course, I asked her to remove it. Uneventfully, she took it off, and I returned to work. All was good.

The next Monday, I was in clinic seeing patients and received a call and a voicemail. It was my dermatologist, who had given me her cell number and asked me to call her back. I stepped outside to make the call, and she said, "Meredith, I am shocked. This is the first time I sent off something that I was not worried about, but sweetie, it is melanoma. Three pathologists have looked at it and graded it 1.7mm deep, which will require a node biopsy as well as a wide excision. Could you come in tomorrow to set up a time with the surgeon?"

I remember sinking to my feet, dumbfounded. Melanoma? What? No one in my family had ever had that, and I knew very little about it. I have never been one to go to the tanning bed and can count on my hand the number of times I was badly burned. I was a lifeguard in high school and enjoy outdoors but have never been a sun-worshipper that I associated with those people who developed melanoma. I went into fix-it mode (like mother, like daughter) and gave myself a pep talk, made the call to my husband, Bruce, and my mom and dad. Throughout the book writing process, the one place I could not let my mind go was that of having a child go through what Mom went through, especially not with my own children. Here, six years later, Mom had begun that dreaded process.

Due to my parents' requests, I called MD Anderson, wanting to get a second opinion and exhaust all options. We had learned firsthand the benefits of second opinions over six years ago. Mom, keeping a close relationship with her medical team there, had e-mailed her oncologist, who promptly responded with a surgeon I needed to see in the melanoma clinic. They actually could see me on Thursday. It was Tuesday.

On Tuesday afternoon, I saw the best surgeon in our hometown of Jackson who recommended the wide excision and sentinel node biopsy, as my dermatologist had thought. He was and is the best around and actually trained at MD Anderson. We tentatively set up the surgery for the next week.

After the adrenaline-filled rush of gathering pathology reports, FedEx-ing the slides from the pathology office, and getting on the road, Bruce and I began that six-hour drive to Houston in a hurry, strikingly similar to Mom and Dad's trip six years before. I remember riding the car, not wanting to talk much, a little upset, but mostly afraid. I told God that I knew He would never give us more than we could handle, and darn, why had I just finished reliving this while putting Mom's book together? Work on her book came to a halt as we refocused to getting this thing behind us.

I saw the surgeon Thursday, who was able to perform the surgery on Friday, the next day. When you hear the dreaded words "It is cancer," no treatment can come fast enough. I was so thankful everything went well, and the surgeon took four lymph nodes for biopsy to make sure nothing had spread.

We waited two weeks on the pathology report—what seemed like an eternity. Each time I called to check on the status of things, I was told that an extreme amount of testing and staining was done to make absolutely sure there are no cancer cells in the lymphatic system. If so, my treatment would consist of more surgery, chemotherapy, and a different prognosis.

After eighteen days, the physician assistant called me to tell me the news that we had convinced ourselves was not true. Two of the four nodes contained microscopic melanoma cells, changing my case to stage three. We returned three weeks later to have my stitches removed and schedule my second surgery, a complete lymphadenectomy of my left groin. I had baseline scans done, CTs of my chest, abdomen, and pelvis, as well as MRI of by brain (which, praise God, showed no other disease in my body) and scheduled with an oncologist who would administer my chemotherapy after the surgery. At the appointment, the surgeon drained 350ccs of fluid, a seroma that had developed at my incision. My leg felt much better. He didn't remove the stitches since my surgery was scheduled for six days later. Bruce and I flew home and tried to be brave.

My children had recently begun walking, and we ran after them everywhere they went. They are hilarious, and in true team fashion, scheme together for each adventure. And everything is an adventure to toddlers! Throughout this entire time, friends and family took turns making sure life stayed stable for us at home. Our nanny, known as SueSue to my kids, selflessly stayed and did whatever needed to be done. My grandparents, Mop and Pop, [and] aunts and uncles came in to help. Our church family rallied and brought meals, came and prayed, bestowed countless blessings we will never forget. We came home from Houston and had a brand new freezer in the garage to hold the meals they provided. My coworkers graciously covered for me and never questioned why things had to happen so quickly.

When we arrived home that night, I noticed my leg was hurting. It had been sore, as expected after surgery, but I remember driving home from the airport and thinking, *Man, that really hurts.* We went to sleep and prepared for another work day. I woke up on Friday morning and felt sick. I called my boss and told him I would be a little late for work and got up, trying to feel better. I began to feel faint and took my temperature, which was over 102. We called MD Anderson, and they advised me to go to the emergency room, that I might have an infection. Turns out, I did have an infection—a bad one.

Talk about feeling out of control. Here I was in the hospital bed with the biggest headache I have ever had, and these new doctors are telling me that I must have surgery now. I thought, *Wait, I am seeing doctors in Houston. I'm supposed to have surgery next week to make sure they get all the cancer. Please don't do anything now. No. No. No.* Doctors who I am privileged to call friends came in to talk sense into me, and the surgeon performed the irrigation and debridement (I&D) that afternoon which revealed a large infection at my surgery site. The wound would have to stay open, and I would have to pack it daily to allow for healing from the inside out. Being a physical therapist, I knew this could take months.

This was the bottom for me. The biggest battle is the daily battle of fear, paralyzing fear. I was afraid that since my big surgery had to be postponed, the cancer continued to rage in my body. I had read how aggressive melanoma is and knew each day was very important. Throughout my journey thus far, I really didn't want anyone to create a Caringbridge or social media webpage for me, as I tried to keep my mind from picturing myself as a cancer patient. I did, however, keep a blog which I felt like was a private way to keep those selflessly praying for me informed. Two days after the surgery for the infection, I lay in the hospital bed, missing my children, and typed an update:

Would you hold, please?

Don't you hate it when someone says that?

Thursday's appointments in Houston went really well. Dr. Ross was very pleased with my scar and how "well I'd healed" and didn't even take the stitches out since surgery was scheduled for the twenty-first. He took some fluid off, which made my leg feel better, and I went on with the day: MRI brain and CTs of chest, abdomen, and pelvis. We flew home Thursday night and crashed.

I got up Friday morning early to get ready for work, got dressed, and felt like I might faint. Told the clinic I'd be a little late and decided to lie down and try to feel better. I called Houston at 8:00 a.m. (Houston, we have a problem) and explained what was going on, and they told me to go straight to the ER, that I might be getting an infection. In other news, the MRI brain and CTs were all good (i.e., no cancer seen there)!

Turns out, yes, a nasty infection had popped up in less than twelve hours. The doctors decided there was no choice Friday afternoon but to have surgery to clean everything out. So darn, looks like everything else will be put on hold for a little while.

As of now, I'm still in the hospital on IV antibiotics, praying the infection begins to subside. I'm also praying MD Anderson will go ahead with the lymph node surgery as soon as possible even though there is a big, open hole in my leg. We know the surgery won't be the twenty-first, as originally planned, but really no idea when it will/can be done. I'm being optimistic and praying hard it'll be done in a week.

I keep looking at Bruce and asking, "Is this really happening?" How could life a month ago be so different? Why in the world do Mr. Melanoma and Mrs. Infection think they have some right to come in and totally disrupt our life? Over the past three whirlwind weeks, I've been reminded many times of the passage in John 9. Jesus and his disciples passed a blind man on the road. The disciples asked Jesus why that man was blind—was it because the man or his parents had sinned? Jesus was quick to answer, "No, of course not." This man is blind so that "the works of God can be displayed in him."

No, cancer is not from God. Neither are holding penalties from infections. (We're watching football right now.) As tempting as it is to dwell on the "why" all is happening, we mustn't. We know the answer: so that God can be glorified. That's all.

The hospital stay lasted six days to get the infection under control; then I was sent home to allow my leg to heal before surgeons in Houston would consider the bigger surgery that was still needed. Thinking back, if I had not had Mom's story for reference, I do not know what I would have done. [Unbeknown] to me, God had been preparing me for this long before. He also provided an undeniable demonstration of His faithfulness and healing in a situation firsthand to me as I watched Him heal my mom. Who am I to fear?

Obvious to many, going through hard times draws us in to focus, and as in previous trials in my life, I spent more time pouring over Scriptures, trying to glean hope, peace, and praying God would cleanse my mind from fear. As psalmists did, we are reminded numerous times to "remember." The Israelites did this daily in the desert, David did this during despair, Paul did this in prison, John did this in exile. Remembering God's miracles and faithfulness not only encourages us, but also brings glory to God. We decided the first day of this new journey that there was no other choice. We must hope. We must trust. I wanted to live.

Romans chapter 4 became my daily reading, particularly verses 20–21: "Yet he did not waver in unbelief regarding the promise of God, but was strengthened in his faith and gave glory to God, being fully persuaded that God had power to do what He has promised." As my mom had prayed, so did I: "Lord, help my unbelief."

And faster than I could have ever imagined, my wound healed, and the surgeon agreed to perform the surgery in Houston November 2, 2011. This turned out to be only a three-week delay from the original surgery date. The plan was to remove all the superficial lymph nodes and test them for any remaining melanoma; of course, my prayer was that this surgery would be done for nothing, that no other melanoma cells would be present, that all were removed with the first surgery.

This surgery was a little more difficult, as I stayed in the hospital four days and had two drains in my leg for five weeks. We got the call about eight days after the surgery, after I was home in Mississippi: all nodes were clear! Praise God! At this point, I remained melanoma stage 3A and need to have chemotherapy and periodic scans to make sure I stay disease-free. Finally, some good news!

I hobbled around for a few weeks, enjoyed Thanksgiving with my family, and returned to Houston after the holiday for removal of the drains and meeting with the oncologist. He recommended interferon alpha, one of the few drugs aside from clinical trials that has shown any success in prolonging recurrence of melanoma. I wanted to begin as soon as possible.

While in the local hospital for my infection, my good friend, Dr. T, who talked sense into me, sent Dr. Y, a local oncologist, into my room. She patiently and clearly explained answers to my questions and compassionately led me to what I believe are the best choices for my treatment. I proudly call her my friend today. She serves as my local oncologist and administered the interferon treatment that I took for one year after my last surgery.

Interferon, as I had been warned, is tough. Melanoma is unlike other cancers that respond to traditional chemotherapy and must be treated with immunotherapy drugs. Interferon is given daily by IV for one month, then injected three times a week for a year, hoping to boost the body's immune system to fight the cancer. The drug hit me hard, but like Mom said, it is a good feeling to know something is working like it should! Thankfully, I was able to continue working the entire year. Most days I simply would get up, go to work, come home, hug my kids, and crash. But truly, you sort of get used to the flu-like symptoms.

In a strange way, the "hit by a truck" feeling that I had the morning after each injection became my comfort in knowing I was doing all I could to prevent any recurrence. I had scans every ninety days to scrutinize my body for any evidence of recurrence, and we had a few scares with enlarged lymph nodes, thyroid nodules, not to mention the mind games Satan plays with the patient day in and day out.

I am now two and a half years from the time of my diagnosis, and while I cannot wait until I get to that pivotal five-year mark,

I do not want to rush things. God has given me the biggest reminder of seizing the day in my larger-than-life children. Time is going by quickly enough!

My advice to the person newly diagnosed is fourfold. Firstly, know to whom you belong. My father instilled this in me as a young girl. How you act is a reflection of who you are as well as to whom you belong. I know I am a child of the King, of God, supreme healer, Jehovah rapha. He has knit me together in my mother's womb and knows all the days written in my book before even one of them came to be (Psalm 139). For by Him, all things were created; He is before all things, and in Him all things hold together (Colossians 1:16–17). His plans for me are good (Jeremiah 29:11). The Lord is my Shepherd. I shall not want (Psalm 23). As is the theme in my mom's story, we belong to Him. Our time here on earth is fleeting and just a blip of time in eternity. Know whose you are, and He will take care of you (Matthew 5).

Secondly, guard your mind and heart. For me, even now, over two years later, fear is my daily battle, my thorn in my side. Who knows? I do know one thing: fear is *not* from God. Some say, "Carry your cross" or "It's your burden." No. I am convinced and God tells me that fear is not from Him. I choose to avoid any trigger in my mind regarding death, sadness, illness, and hurt, including what I read, what I watch, what I talk about. My fear is not only for myself, but for my family and children as well. Satan lurks in the shadow with his daggers of fear, aiming directly for my mind, which is my most vulnerable target. Find what your vulnerability is, and guard it with everything you have.

The best way that I have found to do this is Scripture memory. Some say, "I am just not good at memory; it comes too hard for me." I will testify that memory might seem easier to some than others, but like strength training in the gym, or playing a musical instrument, or even doing math, [it] is improved with deliberate practice. Solomon and David surely understood the benefits and told us to "hide His Word in my heart" and "meditate on it day and night." Scripture is what I repeat over and over in those testing machines.

I laugh when my dad tells me the way he and Mom finally realized how to punish the strong-willed child that I was: I would sit in the basement of my dad's office and write on a yellow legal pad, filling up every single line: "I will not fight about my clothes. I will not fight about my clothes." And they were right; I still remember that to this day! Maybe that's part of the reason I am not the shopper (like Mom told you in the book). Scripture memory and repetition is, for me, one way to meditate on God's promises. As a musician, one of my favorite things about church music is the direct exposition from Scripture. Don't forget, this is also another method of Scripture memory.

Romans 8:6 says, "The mind governed by the flesh is death, but the mind governed by the Spirit is life and peace." To guard the mind while staying focused on the Holy Spirit helps to keep fear at bay and remember peace. Fear presents a bondage that overshadows blessings. I simply cannot be fearful and truly thankful at the same time—period.

Along the same lines, Satan attacks with feelings of loneliness. He knows where our vulnerabilities during hard times lie and won't let them go. Thankfully, we never should be lonely, no matter how it easy it is to feel alone. In fact, John Milton said it so well: "Loneliness is the first thing which God's eye named not good." "Above all else, guard your heart, for it is the wellspring of life" (Proverbs 4:23).

Thirdly, ask questions. Refuse to be a victim. I tell my patients daily, "This is your health. Do not rely on anyone else to tell you what to do. You have options and must make your own decisions.

If you don't feel right about something, ask someone else." Take charge. Do not wait on someone to call you. In my own journey, "I want to live" took on a whole new meaning.

Lastly, rest—easier said than done, right? But this goes back to the first point. Rest in [He to] whom you belong. Life does go on, and nothing will ever be normal again. This is the new normal. But when I look in the mirror and see the scars, I see the new and bigger person I am because of it. Yes, the swelling in my leg, the tight compression hose that I will have to wear forever, and the occasional discomfort will remain. Still, as Sara Groves penned in the song "Taking Pictures of Egypt," "The places that used to fit me cannot hold the things I've learned."

Mercies are new each morning. Let's learn daily together. *Let's live.*

Psalm 91

He who dwells in the shelter of the Most High
Will abide in the shadow of the Almighty.
I will say to the LORD, "My refuge and my fortress,
My God, in whom I trust!"
For it is He who delivers you from the snare of the trapper
And from the deadly pestilence.
He will cover you with His pinions,
And under His wings you may seek refuge;
His faithfulness is a shield and bulwark.
You will not be afraid of the terror by night,
Or of the arrow that flies by day;
Of the pestilence that stalks in darkness,
Or of the destruction that lays waste at noon.
A thousand may fall at your side
And ten thousand at your right hand,
But it shall not approach you.
You will only look on with your eyes
And see the recompense of the wicked.
For you have made the LORD, my refuge,
Even the Most High, your dwelling place.
No evil will befall you,
Nor will any plague come near your tent.

For He will give His angels charge concerning you,
To guard you in all your ways.
They will bear you up in their hands,
That you do not strike your foot against a stone.
You will tread upon the lion and cobra,
The young lion and the serpent you will trample down.

"Because he has loved Me, therefore I will deliver him;
I will set him securely on high, because he has known My name.
"He will call upon Me, and I will answer him;
I will be with him in trouble;
I will rescue him and honor him.
"With a long life I will satisfy him
And let him see My salvation."

Darlene owns Therapy Dynamics, LLC, where she primarily provides consulting to Speech Language Pathologists in schools and to groups involved with preschoolers on pre-literacy skills. She served as President of the MS Speech Language Hearing Association in 2012. She and her daughters are embarking on a new business venture, Essential Play, LLC, which offers monthly toy memberships to children ages birth to four selected by a multidisciplinary team for appropriate play, assisting children to meet their developmental potential.

Darlene serves on the Grenada Arts Partnership Board, the University of Mississippi Alumni Board, and is a member of New Century Book Club. She is a member of First Baptist Church, where she leads a weekly ladies' Bible study.

She plays in a bridge club monthly with ladies she has played with for thirty-six years.

In April, 2011, she was honored as the Woman of Distinction by Grenada Junior Auxiliary.

She is a wonderful grandmother.

Meredith Gore Warf is currently a physical therapist in Jackson, Mississippi, where she works in sports rehabilitation. She is wife to Bruce and mom to Silas and Avery, their 3 1/2 year old twins. Not a day goes by that she isn't thankful for her mom's journey and example of a life worth living.

Resources

Books
So, Stick a Geranium in Your Hat and Be Happy! by Barbara Johnson
The Red Hat Society: fun and friendship after fifty by Sue Ellen Cooper
Humor for a Woman's Heart 2 by Chonda Pierce, Patsy Clairmont, and many more.
Wake Up Laughing—Offbeat devotions for the "unconventional" woman by Rachel St. John-Gilbert (This is my favorite. I laughed out loud when I read this!)
Joy Breaks by Patsy Clairmont, Barbara Johnson, Marilyn Megberg, and Luci Swindoll
When I'm on My Knees by Anita Corrine Donihue
The Prayer That Changes Everything by Stormie Omartian
Why? by Anne Graham Lotz
When God Whispers Your Name by Max Lucado
If You Want to Walk on Water You've Got to Get Out of the Boat by John Ortber
A Bend in the Road by David Jeramiah
The Red Sea Rules by Robert J. Morgan
Discovering God's Will by Jerry Sittser
Just Enough Light for the Step I'm On by Stormie Ormartian
Don't Waste Your Cancer by John Piper

Daily Readings
A chapter in Psalms and another chapter in the New Testament (I went through several books of the Bible.)
Believing God by Beth Moore
Daily devotion by Oswald Chambers: *My Utmost for His Highest*
God Calling by A. J. Russell
Streams in the Desert by L. B. Cowan (This is my favorite, and I still read this book every day.)

Websites

Jesse H. Jones Rotary House: *https://www2.mdanderson.org/sapp/rotaryhouse/*
   800-847-5783
TX Medical Center furnished apartments:
   www.TempStay.com/

Rice Village: *www.ricevillageonline.com*
   Dining, shopping, etc.

Dodie Osteen's Scriptures on healing: *hopefaithprayer.com/?page_id=628*

www.mdanderson.org/patient-and-cancer-information/guide

www.breastcancer.org

www.komen.org

MD Anderson Place of Wellness
http://www.mdanderson.org/education-and-research/departments-programs-and-labs/programs-centers-institutes/place-of-wellness/index.html

MD Anderson publications
http://www.mdanderson.org/publications/index.html

Anderson Network (Connect with another survivor.)
http://www.mdanderson.org/patient-and-cancer-information/guide-to-md-anderson/patient-and-family-support/anderson-network/index.html

Henda
www.densebreasttissue.net

All net proceeds from the sales of this book are dedicated to the Alexa Cooke Foundation at St. Jude Children's Hospital. Alexa fought a courageous battle with osteosarcoma and passed away in 2005, at the young age of 14 years.

CPSIA information can be obtained at www.ICGtesting.com
Printed in the USA
LVOW11s0730011115

460482LV00002B/2/P